Published by
FORMING LIVES INC

Copyright © 2020 by
GOOD WORD TRUST

Title
MY BEST ME - Teacher Guide 4

Editor-In-Chief
Josien Knigge

Author
Heather Long
Anne Marie Wahls
Elizabeth Palmer Solon
Josien Knigge

Editor
Virdeen J. Muñoz

Revision and Correction
Josien Knigge

Technical Editor
Carlos A. Ferrufino

Cover Design
Ziza Zoe Malloy

Special thanks to Dr. Chan Hellman and
the OU-Tulsa Hope Research Center
for their curriculum content review.

HOPE RESEARCH CENTER
The UNIVERSITY of OKLAHOMA - TULSA

ISBN-13: 978-1-951061-19-7

Hope Rising SEL
PO Box 722255
Norman, OK 73070
United States
Tel: (405) 676-4140
Mail: info@hoperisingsel.com
www.hoperisingsel.com

4.0.7. usa

MW01241832

Why My Best Me Works

My Best Me is a series of lessons designed to help young people discover their true identity and purpose. Hope delivered through social emotional learning (SEL) enhances students' cognitive competence giving them the integrated skills needed to deal effectively and ethically with daily tasks and challenges. *My Best Me* integrates intra-personal and interpersonal conversations around five core competencies and seven principles. Student participation, uninterrupted classroom instruction and a superior learning environment are the returns on time invested in hope.

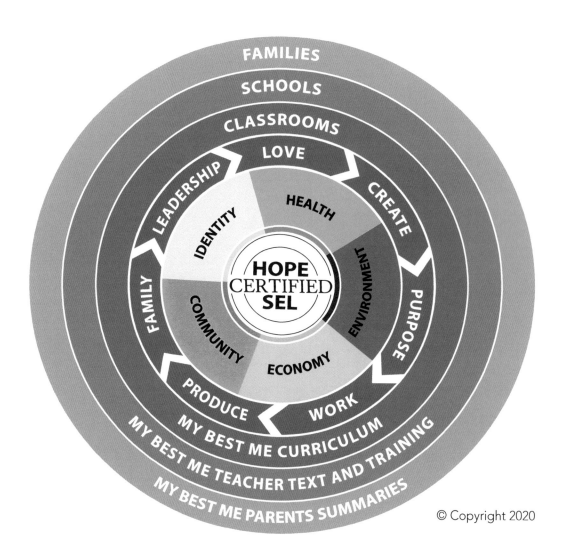

teamwork • willpower • leadership • goal setting • growth mindset • problem solving
time management • reasoning skills • organizing skills • strategic thinking • conflict resolution
willingness to learn • creative thinking • stress management • finance management
communication skills • emotional intelligence • nonverbal communication

The Science and Power of Hope
What Our Research Shows

What is Hope?

Hope is the belief that the future will be better than today, and you play a role in making that future possible. Hope is not a wish. Hope allows us to identify valued goals, set the pathways to achieve those goals, and exert the willpower to make those goals possible.

Can Hope Be Measured?

We published two meta-analytic studies on the Children's Hope Scale and the Adult Hope Scale. These publications provide strong evidence in the validity and reliability of the scales used to measure hope. This research is informing the field that hope scores can be used with confidence for both researchers and practitioners.

Can Hope Be Learned?

This line of research identifies strategies to nurture hope among those experiencing trauma and adversity. Hope is malleable across the life span showing that targeted program services can help move from despair to hope for both children and adults. This research is guiding our work to identify effective practices and develop training programs for service providers.

Impact of Hope on Trauma Survivors:

These publications provide a framework for organizations to become trauma informed and hope centered when working with survivors. Incorporating strategies to nurture hope leads to positive outcomes. This research provides a unifying framework that can shape advocacy and social policy around hope's evidence-based practice.

Impact of Hope on Education Outcomes:

Hope is linked to positive outcomes and important assets:
- Well-Being
- Education: Comparing Lower Hope to Higher Hope Students:
  - Lower Suspension/Expulsion (68% to 91%).
  - Lower Dropout (81%).
  - Lower Chronic Absenteeism (44%).
  - Higher Grades.
  - Higher Graduation Rates.

Chan Hellman PhD

Chan joined the University of Oklahoma in 2002. Chan is a professor in the Anne & Henry Zarrow School of Social Work and Founding Director of the Hope Research Center. He also holds Adjunct Professor appointments in the OU College of Public Health and School of Community Medicine. Chan has numerous scholarly publications and books and has presented his research at both national and international conferences. Chan teaches both the master's and doctoral level primarily in the areas of positive psychology, research methods, and statistics.

Chan's current research is focused on the application of hope theory to predict adaptive behaviors and hope as a psychological strength that buffers stress and adversity among those impacted by family violence. In this context, he is also interested in the impact of prevention and intervention services on improving hope and well-being. Chan has also begun to examine the effects of collective hope on a community's capacity to thrive.

Nurturing HOPE with My Best Me

Schools and classrooms are increasingly filled with children exposed to trauma. Awareness of the impact on the learning environment is increasing and teachers, counselors, and administrators are asking for strategies to work with trauma exposed children. I consistently hear from teachers, that what they need are the tools to mitigate this trauma so that all children in their classroom have the opportunity to thrive. After more than a decade of scientific research, I am convinced that hope is the answer. Children need hope perhaps now more than ever before.

I have been publishing peer-reviewed scientific research studies that demonstrate the simple process to nurture hope in children, youth, and adults. Our research studies have even focused on the impact of hope on children with high trauma experiences such as those described in the Adverse Childhood Experiences (ACE) literature. We have consistently found that nurturing hope in children not only improves their academic performance, but that hope is an important coping resource protecting children from adversity and stress. The science of hope is well-established, demonstrating that hopeful children do better.

Hope is the belief that the future is going to be better than today and that I have the power to make it happen. Hope is not a feeling, but a way of thinking about the future and how you can begin achieving your goals. Hope is the ability to set goals, identify the pathways to achieve those goals, and the capability to focus mental energy (agency) to those pathways. Hope is not wishful thinking, rather, hope is about taking action to pursue your goals. The simplicity of hope is that it is about helping children set goals and finding the pathways and motivation to pursue those goals. The science of hope shows that a child's hope score predicts better grades, attendance, and graduation rates. Classrooms with higher hope children perform better in terms of chronic absenteeism, truancy, drop-out rates, academic achievement, and graduation rates, even when controlling for socioeconomic status. Children with higher hope are better at self-regulating their thoughts, emotions, and behaviors. They are better at setting goals, finding pathways, problem solving, and sustaining the willpower to pursue their goals even when faced with barriers and adversity. Hopeful children have better academic engagement as well as overall well-being. As an added bonus, the science of hope shows that teachers with higher hope are better at finding strategies to reduce burnout and stress so that they may thrive as well.

Hope is good for everyone and is grounded in science. Here is the good news!

1. Hope is a protective factor against anxiety and stress.
2. Hope leads to good outcomes.
3. Hope can be taught and learned.

Improving Hope Through My Best Me

The really exciting news is that hope can be improved through simple learning strategies like those developed in the "My Best Me" curriculum. This research-based curriculum can increase the social and emotional skills that will help nurture and support hope in your classroom. As you go through the curriculum with your students, you will see a greater level of goal setting, pathways development, and sense of agency that is necessary for children to thrive both in and out of the classroom.

As you start to use *My Best Me* to empower students to build their HOPE, here are suggestions for you to begin to build HOPE.

1. To begin this process, start by highlighting core values.
   - Shift the message from avoiding negative behaviors, to achieving what is valued.
   - Discuss the definition of hope and how it differs from wishful thinking
   - Connect each individual to a greater sense of belonging and achievement.

2. Practice short-term goal setting.
   - Trauma exposed children are much better at short-term thinking.
   - List the short-term benchmarks as steps toward your goal.
     1. What can you do this week, today, this hour, this moment?

3. Actions should be inspirational. Pathways that clearly connect to the goal are motivating and show children that their future is possible.

4. Set up processes to capture and share stories about **hope heroes**, people who find creative solutions to barriers to achieving their dream. (Hope Modeling).

5. Stay connected: Hope is a social gift that is nurtured through relationships.

6. When we experience adversity, trauma leads us to worry about the future or ruminate on the past. When our attention is focused on worry or rumination, we cannot be enthusiastic about the future.

7. Hope is a candle in the darkness. Create a Hope Map or simple visual to communicate hope to others.
   - Use pictures or symbols that provide a visual for goals, pathways, agency that can be displayed in the classroom.
   - Visual maps are a daily reminder that our future is possible

To learn more about HOPE, how it is measured, and strategies to nurture in children and adults, read *HOPE Rising, How the Science of HOPE Can Change Your Life* by Casey Gwinn, J.D. and Chan Hellman, Ph.D.

Contents

 Identity

Health

Community

Environment

Economics

Understanding the Icons

 READ

A story, a poem, a saying or a script that adds to the subject

 APPLY

To bring into action, put to use, and demonstrate understanding

 UNDERSTAND

To obtain knowledge, insight, and understanding through information

 GIFT

A contribution, present or surprise to share with others

 OBSERVE

To look, see, find, watch, and discover more

 ACTIVITY

A task that involves direct experience and action

 CREATE

To paint, color or make in a personal manner

 COMMENT

Discuss, consider, or examine certain subjects

 GAME

Engage in an experience and discovery together

 REFLECT

Think, ponder, meditate or wonder about important issues

 WRITE

To write, mark, or sketch personal ideas or discoveries

 MUSIC

To learn, write, sing or listen to a song; enjoy a harmony of sounds

 CONCLUSION

A closing statement on the lesson subject with a final thought

 VIDEO

Watch a clip or film section and analyze the information

Materials
Writing utensils, journal and/or paper for writing, *My Best Me* textbook, audiovisual equipment

Resources
Introduction Parent: 4yu.info/?i=98540
Student Worksheet: 4yu.info/?i=98401
Parent Summary: 4yu.info/?i=98451
Student Pledge: 4yu.info/?i=98541
Video: Hope Works Link - 4yu.info/?i=94011

Glossary
confidentiality

Motivation
Hope is the assurance that the future is going to be better than today and that you, personally, have the power within you to make it happen.

Hope is not a feeling, but a way of thinking about the future and your role in achieving your goals. Hope is the ability to set goals, identify the pathways to achieving those goals, and the capability to act on those pathways. Hope is not wishful thinking; rather, hope is about taking action in pursuit of your goals. The beauty of hope is that it is teachable and, therefore, measurable.

When we understand that increased hope levels predict greater and better outcomes of success and that the steps to increasing our hope are so simple, hope should arise. *My Best Me* is a tool in your hand to support your students in building their hope through a social emotional learning process.

1

Why My Best Me?

Goal To discover the power of HOPE and why I need it

Pathways

Read - A short story by anonymous
"Thanksgiving Day was near. A first grade teacher gave her class an assignment to draw a picture of something for which they were thankful. Many would celebrate the holiday with turkey and other traditional goodies. These, the teacher thought, would be the subjects of most of her student's art, and they were. But Douglas made a different kind of picture. Douglas was a different kind of boy. He was timid, frail and withdrawn. As other children played at recess, Douglas was likely to stand close by the teacher's side. One could only guess at the pain Douglas felt behind those sad eyes.

Yes, his picture was different. Douglas drew a hand. Nothing else. Just an empty hand. His abstract image captured the imagination of his peers. Whose hand could it be? One child guessed it was the hand of a farmer, because they raise turkeys. Another suggested a police officer, because they protect and care for people. Still others guessed it was the hand of God, for God feeds us. And so the discussion went until the teacher almost forgot the young artist himself. When the children had gone on to other assignments, she paused at Douglas' desk, bent down, and asked him whose hand it was. The little boy looked away and muttered, It's yours, teacher.

She recalled the times she had taken his hand and walked with him here or there, as she had the other students. How often had she said, Take my hand, Douglas, we'll go outside. Or, Let me show you how to hold your pencil. Or, Let's do this together. Douglas was most thankful for his teacher's hand. Brushing aside a tear, she went on with her work."

Comment
What did the teacher's hand mean for Douglas?
Did Douglas need hope in his life?
Why do you think he needed hope?

Observe
Look at page 3. You can build hope in your life in 3 simple steps:
1. _____

10

Goal

Students will be introduced to the concept of hope to discover its power and why it is important to their lives

Pathways

Read: Have a student read this section or give students opportunities to read one sentence at a time. It is a story of a young boy who needed willpower to accomplish simple goals like going outside, and how his teacher provided a pathway of support for him to reach that goal.

Comment: The focus of these questions is to understand how hope can be defined in this short story. Have students put into words how they see hope in this story. In our society, we often hear the

2. _____
3. _____

Understand

The *My Best Me* lessons are openly discussed in class and at home. Some lessons might cause you to feel uncomfortable. This is not unusual because lessons can be very personal. If you or your classmates experience any uncomfortable feelings, write it down and/or talk about it with your teacher, counselor, parent or guardian. It is healthy to talk about things that worry you with someone you trust. Here are some steps to enjoy the lessons:

- Be active and participate. You are building a better future for yourself and others.
- Be kind and thoughtful. Treat others the way you would like to be treated.
- Be trustworthy. Be a person that others trust with personal information.
- Be wise. Know that sometimes it is best to only trust an adult.
- Be a hope giver. Be someone who always helps others find hope and a better future.

Apply

Your teacher will ask everyone in your class to sign a <u>Confidentiality</u> Agreement. That means that everyone promises to actively participate in class, be kind, thoughtful, trustworthy and wise. You are encouraged to sign this Agreement and build hope.

Video: 4yu.info/?i=94011

Watch this clip on how to make your life better and share your thoughts with the class.

4yu.info/?i=94011

Reflect

Do you think you have hope? Please explain.
Do you think you can increase your hope? How?

Willpower

I have hope because I set and achieve my goals through the pathways I choose and the willpower I develop.

---

word "hope" used, but generally, it is used in terms of wishful thinking, which is not the true definition of hope.

Observe: Students will be encouraged to take some time to page through the *My Best Me* textbook and discover what it is about. To help them in this process, they will need to find the definition of hope in their textbook on pages 2 and 3. Have them write down the 3 simple steps of hope. (Set goals, find pathways and build willpower).

Understand: Because these lessons are addressing social emotional learning, expect emotions to surface in some or maybe all or your students and that social frictions might occur during some of these lessons. That is exactly what the *My Best Me* lessons are meant to address, the development of the social and emotional skills necessary to facilitate academic learning. It is wise to be prepared and understand the emotional condition of your class on the days that you go through these lessons. If you sense possible frictions, organize your class in such a manner that you will be able to manage your students and their reactions.

Encourage your students to enjoy these lessons by applying the 5 points addressed in this section. Take time to review these points with your students and remind them that these are your expectations of them each day throughout the year.

Apply: Because of the sensitive issues that will be addressed and the information some of the students might share with the class, a Confidentiality Agreement (student pledge) has been attached (see link: 4yu.info/?i=98541) This agreement is an invitation to students to commit to being a trustworthy classmate by honoring others and what they share.

Video: Have your students watch this beautiful clip on Hope Works. It is very inspirational. Allow them to share their thoughts, ideas and emotions with the class.

Reflect: This is an opportunity to consider if what the students learned in this lesson changed their perspective on hope. Encourage students to immediately apply small steps of hope in their life. Ask them to identify a goal they can set for themselves, along with some steps they can take now toward that goal.

Willpower

Ask the students to read the willpower statement aloud together, reinforcing its truth to themselves. If you notice that some did not participate, enthusiastically encourage all to read aloud together a second time.

Lesson 2

Materials

My Best Me textbook, writing utensils, crayons, one balloon for each student, pictures or photos of themselves from home. (If a student does not have access to their pictures, invite them to find images on line or to bring images of the different stages of life of other people.)

Resources

Student Worksheet: 4yu.info/?i=98402
Parent Summary: 4yu.info/?i=98452

Glossary

appreciate, sequence, hormones, chemical, insecure, embarrassed, maturing, responsibilities

Motivation

The purpose of this lesson is to help young students understand that their bodies, emotions, and thinking processes are constantly changing as they mature and become older.

These changes are not only a natural part of life, but also a necessary part of growing up. The students may feel uncomfortable or embarrassed about these changes, and might find it hard to talk about them.

Help your students understand that these changes happen at different rates for each individual, and that it's important to accept and appreciate the changes that they will go through in life, knowing that every person goes through the same changes. Your ability to normalize and help students understand these changes will better prepare them to cope as they go through these different phases. You can explain the commonality of these changes by giving examples of how many changes take place in our bodies in one day (cells dying off, organs fulfilling their functions, etc.). Ideally, you want to create such clarity that students understand that there is no reason to be embarrassed or self-conscious. It is a normal part of maturing and getting older.

2 Change: An Important Part of Life

Goal
To appreciate the growth process that I go through in life

Pathways

 Write
Sequence these pictures using the numbers 1 - 4.

_____   _____   _____   _____

 Comment
How are the pictures similar? How are they different?
What can you do now that you could not do when you were younger?
What might you like to do in the future that you can not do now?
How do you recognize physical growth? Mental growth? Emotional growth?

 Understand
We are always growing and changing, which is an important part of life. As we grow, we will experience certain changes in our bodies as a result of hormones. Hormones are like chemical messengers in our body. They tell our body when it's time to change and how to change. Sometimes these changes can cause us to have many different emotions. Sometimes we might feel uncomfortable in our bodies,

(12)

Goal

Students will understand and learn to appreciate the changes and growth they go through in life. Read the goal aloud and ask the class what it means

Pathways

Write: The students will observe the four pictures in the workbook, which show a female at different stages of life. They will sequence the pictures in the correct order by numbering each image below the picture. They should be able to write down the reasons for the sequence they chose.

Comment: Ask students to share how the pictures of the female are similar, and how they are different. You can make two lists on the white board. Next, have students share examples of how they

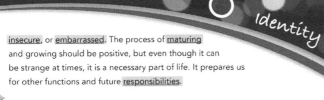

insecure, or embarrassed. The process of maturing and growing should be positive, but even though it can be strange at times, it is a necessary part of life. It prepares us for other functions and future responsibilities.

Activity
On a separate piece of paper, make a time line of your life showing the changes you have gone through and the changes that are ahead. You can draw, write and/or paste images to show your growth and development.

Apply
1. Each student gets a balloon.
2. When your teacher says go, you will blow up your balloon until you hear the signal to stop.
3. Once you hear the stop signal, hold the balloon over your head.
4. Look around at all of your classmates' balloons.

Reflect
How did inflating the balloons make them change?
Did all the balloons inflate at the same rate?
What might have caused the balloons to expand at different rates?
What kind of growth have I been experiencing (looking at my time line)?
What part of my growth was the most exciting and fun for me?
Why do I need to grow and change?
How do I feel about the growth and changes I'm going through?
What are 3 things I appreciate in my life at this moment?

Willpower
I appreciate and am excited about the changes that I am going through in life.

13

themselves have changed throughout their life so far. These changes can be: physical changes (getting taller or stronger); emotional changes (becoming more self-conscious); or changes in their thinking process, skills or abilities. For example, they might have cried because they were afraid of the dark when they were younger, but now they are brave and no longer cry. Talk with the students about how and why these changes are important in life. What would happen if we never changed?

 Understand: Read this together. Talk with the students about growth and what it means; why living creatures grow and change. Explain to them how our hormones function as chemical messengers in our bodies, telling it when it is time to change, and also how to change. As we get older, our hormones adjust, as well as our bodies, our emotions and our behavior. Discuss with the students how they might be feeling as they change. Some of the changes might seem weird or awkward, but it is something that is a natural part of life.

Activity: Previous to this lesson, ask the students to bring in a few pictures of themselves (or others) at different ages in their lives. They will use the images to make a time line of their own life. If some students do not bring pictures, they can simply draw their own or use the pictures they brought of other people. They will glue the pictures in order on a piece of paper. Under each picture, the students can identify the age depicted.

This activity will be a visual for students to see how much they have changed in their lives so far. Encourage the students to go deeper by looking at more than just their physical changes. Invite them to write a paragraph reflecting on how their thoughts and interests have changed and what the future looks like in their imagination. Allow students to share their time line and get to know each other better.

Apply: This activity will help students visualize different growth rates for different people. On the signal of the teacher, students will start to blow up the balloon they have been given. They will stop when instructed. Students will hold up their balloons and compare them with each other. Ask students to observe the differences; some may be large while others are fairly small. The balloons, can be compared to the students. Even though the students are all the same age, they are all growing and changing at different rates.

Reflect: The balloon activity can lead to a conversation about some of the changes that students are experiencing. Talk with them about how these changes affect them and their life. Can the students imagine what would happen if we never changed and always stayed the same?

Willpower

Have the students read the willpower statement aloud together.

15

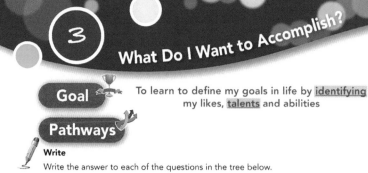

Lesson 3

Materials

My Best Me textbook, writing utensils, letter-writing paper, an envelope for each student
* Suggestion: a good book you could use is *Oh, the Places You Will Go!* by Dr. Seuss.

Resources

Student Worksheet: 4yu.info/?i=98403
Parent Summary: 4yu.info/?i=98453
Article: Dreams: 4yu.info/?i=94021

Glossary

identifying, talents, achieving, excel, destiny, tendency, chef, recipes, flavors, symbol, nutrients, nourish, accomplishments, short-term, long-term, series, safekeeping

Motivation

We want to help the students think about their future and what dreams they would like to accomplish. Dreams are powerful; John Maxwell in his book *The Road Map to Success*, says concerning dreams, "... I'm talking about a vision deep inside that speaks to the very soul. It's the thing we were born to do. It draws on our talents and gifts. It appeals to our highest ideals. It sparks our feelings of destiny. It is inseparably linked to our purpose in life. The dream starts us on the success journey." (4yu.info/?i=94021). Maxwell goes on to explain in his book how dreams:
• work like a compass, giving direction as to where we are headed, starting from where we are right now;
• increase and reveal our potential because we discover the resources within ourselves;
• help us prioritize and focus in on what we want to accomplish;
• add value and significance to what we are doing because they create space for our emotional involvement;
• predict our future, because of who we become as we pursue the fulfillment of our dreams.

Have students reflect upon their dreams, so they discover what makes them happy, as well as identifying their talents and abilities.

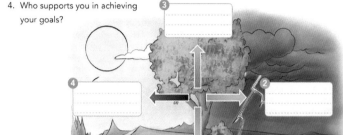

3 · What Do I Want to Accomplish?

Goal To learn to define my goals in life by identifying my likes, talents and abilities

Pathways

Write

Write the answer to each of the questions in the tree below.
1. What do you dream of being when you are older?
2. What obstacles/challenges must you overcome before achieving your goals?
3. What areas do you excel in?
4. Who supports you in achieving your goals?

Understand

We are born with interests, talents and abilities that can guide and drive us to achieve our goals and reach our destiny. For example, a person who likes to cook will probably have a tendency to learn more on this subject, try out what they have learned, and might eventually even become a (master) chef. They probably enjoy looking at new recipes, cooking shows, studying techniques, or experimenting with different flavors in order to develop their talent.

14

Goal

Students will learn to define what they want to do with their lives by analyzing their interests and utilizing their talents and abilities

Pathways

Write: Students will write their answers to the questions on the tree in the workbook. Each question is numbered corresponding to the blank spaces on the tree, which are numbered as well. Encourage the students to think about these questions, talk them through with a classmate (if helpful), and answer them honestly.

Understand: Although it is not necessary for 4th-grade students to make any decisions about their future, it is helpful for them to start thinking about what interests them, what areas they are successful in, and

The image of the tree on page 14 is a <u>symbol</u> of our life. There is a stormy side and a sunny side. These different sides represent the changes and growth we will go through on the road to our goals. The stormy side of the tree represents some of the difficulties or obstacles we might encounter, while the sunny side represents the support we receive from others on our journey. The roots of the tree represent the <u>nutrients</u> we need to realize our dreams, which are our talents, interests and knowledge, because they <u>nourish</u> our <u>accomplishments</u>. The green branches are the things we achieve and the impact we have on others.

Think about your goals, both <u>short-term</u> and <u>long-term</u>. A short-term goal is something you want to accomplish within a few days or weeks. A long-term goal is something that will take longer, maybe a year to accomplish. Develop a plan and a <u>series</u> of short-term goals that will help you achieve your long-term goals. For example: If your long-term goal is to join the school soccer team, you could set a short-term goal of running three times per week and practice kicking goals for 30 minutes each day. Write down your goals and review them every day. Celebrate when you successfully complete them.

Activity

Write a letter that you would like to give to yourself 20 years from today. In this letter, describe in detail how you see your future self. What will your life look like? What will you have accomplished? Who will you have impacted? Once it is done, give it to someone for <u>safekeeping</u>. Have this person give the letter back to you somewhere in the future.

Reflect

Do I know what I would like to accomplish?
Do I have a plan to achieve my dreams?
Do I need help from other people? If so, from whom?
What brings true happiness in life? Why?

Willpower

I define my goals by focusing on my interests and analyzing my strengths and abilities.

15

The green leaves at the top of the tree are their accomplishments and their impact on others. The dark side of the tree is the obstacles they may face, while the sunny side of the tree represents the people who will help encourage and support them along the way. Make sure the students understand how all the different parts of the tree are related and play an important role in shaping their future. Students might want to add other aspects that influence their development to the tree. Be sure to create space for their ideas.

Activity: The goal is for the students to write a letter to their future self. The students will write in detail about the life they want to be living in 20 years. First, ask the students how old they will be at the time. What goals would they like to have accomplished? What do they think their lives might look like? How would they like to describe themselves? How may they have impacted others along the way? Once your students know the expectation, give them a piece of paper to write their letter. After writing their letters, allow them to share what they are feeling after going through this exercise. Once they are finished sharing, have the students put their letters into an envelope to take home and give to someone for safe keeping.

Reflect: After writing the letters, close the lesson by discussing the reflection questions in the workbook as a class. At the end of the lesson, the students should have a better understanding of their strengths and abilities and how they will help shape their future. True happiness exists in sharing moments of life with others.

---

how they can further develop those areas. It is powerful for them to write down their thoughts and imaginations. Emphasize that it is okay to change direction during this process of discovery and growth; sometimes we develop different interests or discover new hobbies or talents. Students should realize that there is power in pursuing their dreams and doing what truly gives them joy.

Read this section of the workbook together. Then have students share their goals with their classmates. Discuss with them what talents they have, and how they plan to foster those talents to help them reach their goals. Some ideas might be to practice their skills, take an extra class in that area, go to college, etc.

Next, have the students go back to the tree in the workbook. Explain to them that the tree represents their life and what they desire to accomplish. The roots are what keeps the tree in the ground and assures its growth. This represents the students' dreams and visions tied to their interests and talents, rooted in their core convictions. This is what is going to guide, direct and support them as they move toward their destiny.

Willpower

Ask for 2 or 3 volunteers to read the Willpower statement aloud together. Ask for a show of hands from those who learned something during the lesson. Ask them what they learned.

Lesson 4

Materials
My Best Me textbook, writing utensils, journal, paper, yellow and blue crayons for each student

Resources
Student Worksheet: 4yu.info/?i=98404
Parent Summary: 4yu.info/?i=98454

Glossary
promptly, procrastination, proactive, momentum, domino effect, defeated, determination, grit, initiative, passive, postpone, decisively

Motivation
The purpose of this lesson is for students to understand the difference between passive and assertive behavior. When we are passive, we procrastinate on projects or ideas and slack in our responsibilities, so they do not get done properly or in a timely manner. When we are assertive and take initiative, we are responsible and accomplish and complete the tasks and jobs that are at hand.

When tasks are not completed on time, we let ourselves and others down. Learning to take initiative, act and complete tasks in a timely manner is an important skill that students will use throughout their entire lives. We can start teaching students at a young age to be assertive learners, especially in classroom settings and with their homework assignments.

This might mean helping students break down projects into smaller pieces to complete them on time, writing important deadlines in an agenda or calendar, or practicing solid and efficient study habits. When we teach students to become assertive, they will be more successful in school and life.

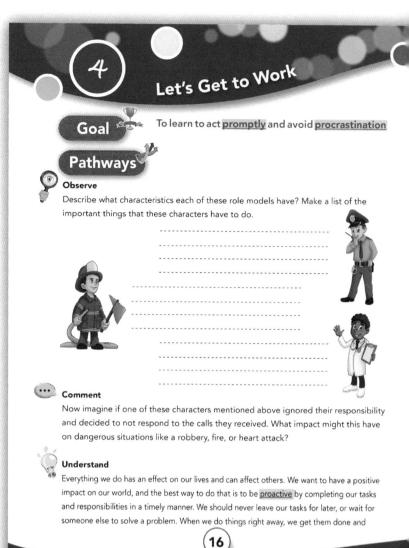

Let's Get to Work

4

Goal To learn to act promptly and avoid procrastination

Pathways

Observe
Describe what characteristics each of these role models have? Make a list of the important things that these characters have to do.

Comment
Now imagine if one of these characters mentioned above ignored their responsibility and decided to not respond to the calls they received. What impact might this have on dangerous situations like a robbery, fire, or heart attack?

Understand
Everything we do has an effect on our lives and can affect others. We want to have a positive impact on our world, and the best way to do that is to be proactive by completing our tasks and responsibilities in a timely manner. We should never leave our tasks for later, or wait for someone else to solve a problem. When we do things right away, we get them done and

16

Goal

Students will learn to act in a healthy and timely manner. They should understand that they themselves are the key to their future and who they grow into

Pathways

Observe: The students will look at the characters, "hero figures" in our daily life that are key to our wellbeing when we need their help. After identifying the characters, the students will list some of the important things that each of these characters accomplish in their respective roles.

Comment: After identifying the role models, have the students imagine that these people become angry and frustrated one day and don't want to do anything. How would our community be impacted by

put an energy into motion that will build up momentum and have a powerful effect on everyone involved. However, when we procrastinate by putting things off, often, tasks are not done correctly, which can create a domino effect of feeling frustrated and defeated, as well as exposing ourselves and others to danger or loss. One idea, followed by action, determination, and grit (a tough mindset that never gives up) can change the world!

Activity

Color the pictures yellow that show a situation in which someone is showing initiative and taking action. Color the pictures blue that show someone showing passive behavior.

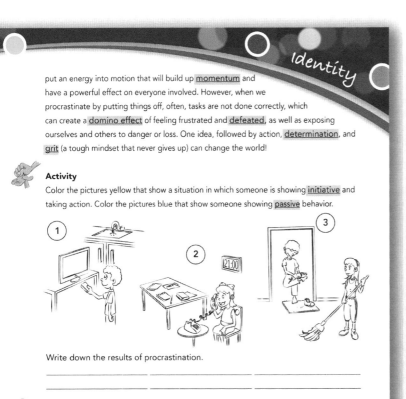

Write down the results of procrastination.

_____ _____ _____
_____ _____ _____

Reflect

Describe a time when you procrastinated.
Why did you postpone doing the work that needed to be done?
Describe a situation in which you showed initiative. What resulted from this good effort?

Willpower

I act promptly and decisively to accomplish the tasks and jobs that need to be done.

17

their passive behavior of doing nothing? The goal is for the students to see and understand that the outcome of their negligent behavior would drastically effect the wellbeing of others.

Understand: Read this section together. Talk with the students about the difference between being passive and being assertive and proactive. For example, if you do not understand your math homework, you could be passive; just trying it on your own or not doing it at all or you could be assertive, going on-line to research the answer or asking a classmate for help. The person who takes initiative and actively—with determination—searches for ways to accomplish the task, will have a better outcome than the person who does not. When we have an idea, assertiveness can transform that idea into a tangible reality.

You could role play school situations in which students are being both passive and assertive. Some example situations could be: starting a science project; studying for a test; participating in a reading circle; putting away supplies in an orderly fashion.

Activity: The three pictures are meant to demonstrate the difference between passive and assertive behaviors. Once the class has discussed these pictures, they can draw the outcomes of each of the situations in the space provided in the workbook. This will help them see that assertive behavior usually has a better outcome than passive behavior. Allow them to talk about the outcome of each situation and focus on the consequences and what might happen in the future as a result.

You can also focus this activity on some simple changes you might wish to see in the classroom. Through questions, guide the students to discover the improvements you believe would impact a better learning environment. Then ask them what assertive behavior could bring change to that situation.

Reflect: The students can verbally answer these questions, or complete them in their journal individually. Once done, they can share their reflections with a partner, or as a class. Encourage students to be honest with themselves as they reflect on those areas where procrastination or passivity may be an issue for them (e.g., efficient hygiene habits, doing chores at home, practicing a skill, doing homework, etc.) They will also identify areas in which they are assertive or show initiative, and the positive results of such actions. This might be in the classroom, playing a sport, or practicing a skill. Let their experience be their teacher.

Willpower

Have the students write the Willpower statement somewhere: a piece of paper, in their phone, on their tablet, on their book cover, on the board, etc. Once everyone has written it twice, have everyone read it aloud together.

Lesson 5

Materials
My Best Me textbook, writing utensils, blank paper for writing, access to Internet

Resources
Student Worksheet: 4yu.info/?i=98405
Parent Summary: 4yu.info/?i=98455

Glossary
leaning, bifocal glasses, personality traits, persevere, Growth Mindset, advantage, overcomer

Motivation
Students should realize that they have strengths and weaknesses in their personalities. As they define these areas in their lives, they will gain greater clarity about their future, what they want to accomplish, and their dreamed-of destiny. Students should understand why it's important to pinpoint and develop one's strengths, as it is a direct road to future success.

Your students will have varying levels of confidence. Some will believe they are very capable in most things, while others will have the idea that they are failures. The good news is that we have the opportunity to teach them a valuable truth: failure is not defined by falling down, but by deciding to stay down when we fall. And even more encouraging is the fact that if you flounder, but then get up, that is a success. It is important for students to learn this because they are at the age in which they are going to start comparing their abilities to those of their peers.

Students will notice some things are difficult for them. Nevertheless, they will still need to do their best. This creates the opportunity to recognize that where they are weak, someone else is strong. Students will learn to work with that person to strengthen the weak spots in themselves. Teach students to lean on their strengths while discovering their weaknesses. We do want to encourage them to always do things to the best of their ability and knowledge.

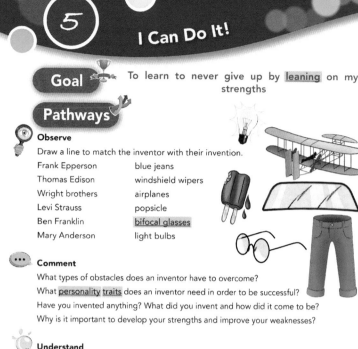

Goal To learn to never give up by leaning on my strengths

Pathways

🔍 **Observe**
Draw a line to match the inventor with their invention.

Frank Epperson	blue jeans
Thomas Edison	windshield wipers
Wright brothers	airplanes
Levi Strauss	popsicle
Ben Franklin	bifocal glasses
Mary Anderson	light bulbs

💬 **Comment**
What types of obstacles does an inventor have to overcome?
What personality traits does an inventor need in order to be successful?
Have you invented anything? What did you invent and how did it come to be?
Why is it important to develop your strengths and improve your weaknesses?

💡 **Understand**
In life, we are always learning and growing as individuals. Our attitude in each situation can affect things negatively or positively. Some of the goals we set will be easy to reach, while others will be more difficult. If we learn to control our frustrations and persevere no matter what, we move forward. After 1,000 unsuccessful attempts at creating a light bulb, a reporter asked Thomas Edison, "How did it feel to fail 1,000 times?" The inventor replied, "I didn't fail 1,000 times. The light bulb was an invention with 1,000 steps."

Our strengths help us to find success. Those victories inspire us to reach for other goals. As we press forward goal after goal, learning from our mistakes instead of being stopped

18

Goal

Students will learn how important it is to persevere, lean on their strengths and work together with others

Pathways

🔍 **Observe:** The students will use their background knowledge to try and match the invention with the inventor. It is okay if they do not know the answers; just encourage the students to guess.

Go over their answers as a class. You might encourage them to break up in small groups, assign each one an invention and ask them to read about the inventor. This will give students insight that these people were not much different from them. If they could do it back then with less resources and access to information, your

by them, we develop a <u>Growth Mindset</u>. This simply means that we never stop believing in the ability of our brain to learn and our efforts to succeed. (We will explore Growth Mindset in detail in Lesson 10.) When recognize our areas of strength, we can use them to our <u>advantage</u>. When we see areas of weakness, we can connect with others to support us and help us to build up those areas. Life is teamwork, and we all need each other to reach our goals.

 Write

Make a list of your strengths. Next to each strength, write a plan on how you will further develop these skills.

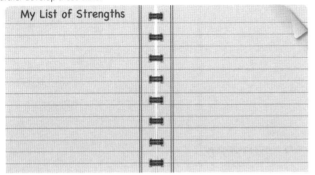

My List of Strengths

 Reflect

What personality trait makes me feel most successful?
Why is it important to develop my strengths and improve my weaknesses?
How do I see others helping me in my areas of weakness?

 Willpower

I am an <u>overcomer</u>! I focus on my strengths to persevere and succeed.

19

An inventor is creative and persistent. Edison did not give up on designing the light bulb; no matter how often he made a mistake, he refused to stop and kept finding new ways until he finally created what he had in mind. Often, it takes many tries to get something just right. It can be a frustrating process to invent something; the reward, though, makes it worth the struggle.

Take some time to talk about what success looks and feels like and what it really is. Being successful is challenging. However, focusing on our strengths will help us reach our full potential. Invite students to share a success in their past that they achieved because they would not give up. (e.g., riding a bike, learning to skate, learning to read, etc.). Share your own experiences as well.

Write: The students will make a list of their strengths or areas of success. Next to each strength, the student will write ways that they can foster these skills to improve and become more successful. Students should understand that to have personality weaknesses can actually be a positive; it shows us the areas in our life in which we will need to learn to lean on others. No one can do everything very well. Working together with others will improve the outcome and make us grow stronger. In fact, even in our areas of weakness, we should still put forth our best effort and willpower.

Reflect: Emphasize that personality is different from character. Personality is based on inner traits, while character is how we use those traits to affect our circumstances.

---

students can invent something today. The answers: Frank Epperson - Popsicle; Thomas Edison - light bulb; Wright Brothers - airplane; Ben Franklin - bifocal glasses; Levi Strauss - blue jeans: Mary Anderson - windshield wipers.

Comment: The students can discuss in small groups each of the inventions and the success of the inventors. Encourage them to talk about how their inventions effected the way we live. Some inventions greatly impact our daily lives, like the invention of electricity or the automobile, while others have less of an impact but are fun or handy to have, such as a paper clip, color pencils and donuts. Have the students think about what invention has impacted their lives the most. Encourage the students to talk about the invention process. Is it easy or difficult to invent something brand new? Have any of the students ever invented something?

Understand: Read this section of the workbook together. Anyone can be an inventor. When we see something that is not working efficiently or effectively, we can invent a solution to fix that problem.

Willpower

Have the students read the Willpower statement aloud together, then quickly go around the room so each student can say a one-word strength they possess.

21

Lesson 6

Materials
My Best Me textbook, writing utensils, materials to make a game: construction paper, markers, crayons, dice, game pieces, origami papers, etc., audiovisual equipment

Resources
Student Worksheet: 4yu.info/?i=98406
Parent Summary: 4yu.info/?i=98456
Video: 4yu.info/?i=94051

Glossary
effectively, origami, alternative, communicate, transferring, relaying, focused, gear, engaged, interview

Motivation
Students will learn about the importance of communicating in clear, effective ways, both verbally and non-verbally. We have to be able to actively and openly listen to others as well as know how to wait our turn to speak. If we are able to communicate effectively, we can solve any problem.

To hear another person, you must employ active listening, which means we participate in the conversation. Others can tell we are actively listening when we look them in the eyes while they are speaking, nod our heads in agreement, emotionally react to the things they say, or briefly repeat what was said. When we actively listen, the person with whom we are communicating will feel that we not only heard what they said, but that we understand why they said it. They will feel valued and be more inclined to listen to what we have to say, because we have respected their ideas by listening.

Sometimes with all of the distractions and technology around us, it is hard to actively listen. We might hear someone talk, but without actively listening, we probably don't comprehend what they say. When we do not listen, we may hurt someone's feelings or miscommunicate with them. Challenge each student to become an active listener in the classroom when others are talking.

Goal To learn how and why to communicate effectively

Pathways

Create
Do your best and create a board or card game to share with your classmates. Make sure to include:
- a game board or game cards
- game pieces
- directions

Once your game is created, invite your classmates to play your game!

Watch Video: (Instructions) 4yu.info/?i=94051
Option: Use origami as an alternative activity; help one another with folding your paper into an animal.

4yu.info/?i=94051

Comment
Was it easy or difficult to play your game (or make origami) with your classmate(s)?
How did you communicate the directions to your classmate(s)?
Were any of the directions of the activity unclear? How did you solve this problem?
How could you have improved your communications with your partner?

Understand
There are three parts to communication: the sender, the message and the receiver. All three parts are important. Communication is transferring information from one person to another. When we communicate with someone, we need to make sure our message is delivered clearly. The person who is speaking is responsible for relaying the message.

20

Goal

Students will learn how and why to communicate effectively. Invite the students to go into more detail once you have read the goal aloud

Pathways

Create: Give students in small groups time to create a game; a board or card game that they can play with other students. If the task seems too big for the student, have them regroup or do the origami activity. Ask students to think about some of their favorite games and what parts and directions are needed to play them, such as a game board, cards, game pieces, a start and finish, directions, etc.

Allow students to playing their games in small groups. The purpose of this lesson is to learn the value

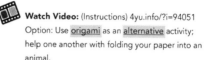

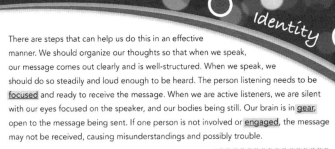

There are steps that can help us do this in an effective manner. We should organize our thoughts so that when we speak, our message comes out clearly and is well-structured. When we speak, we should do so steadily and loud enough to be heard. The person listening needs to be focused and ready to receive the message. When we are active listeners, we are silent with our eyes focused on the speaker, and our bodies being still. Our brain is in gear, open to the message being sent. If one person is not involved or engaged, the message may not be received, causing misunderstandings and possibly trouble.

 Activity - Interview
Write three questions you would like to ask a classmate to better understand who he/she is. Interview your classmate by asking them the questions. Listen actively to their answers!

 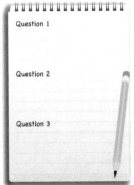

Question 1

Question 2

Question 3

 Reflect
How can I be sure that I am communicating clearly with other people?
Have I ever experienced unclear communications from other people?
What did I observe in those situations?
Why are some people's communications easier to understand than others?
What is one thing I need to improve in my communication style?

 Willpower
I can communicate effectively by sending clear, thoughtful messages and listening actively.

21

---

of communicating effectively, hence, the need to create instructions. The students will see very quickly that if they are not able to communicate well, their games won't be successful.

 Comment: After the students have had a chance to play their games, have them reflect on how the communications worked; what was understood and what was missed? Were the students able to convey the instructions clearly? Were their peers listening to how to play the games properly? Teach students to take responsibility, rather than blaming anyone. Was there effective communication? If they believe errors were made, teach them to use "I statements" tied to "when." (I was confused when... , I felt uncomfortable when ... etc.) Talk about how and why miscommunication happen.

Understand: The goal is for students to understand the different aspects of communication. There are three important parts: the messenger (sender), the message (what and how something is said), and the receiver (listener). Help them understand that when they

send a message, they need to package the information correctly, and confirm that the person they are talking to is listening and receiving what is said.

You can show the students an example by rambling on for a few minutes about something that is irrelevant to them while they are all doing something else. Then review with them what just happened.

Next, describe an active, effective listener; they have their voice quiet, ears listening, eyes looking at the speaker, and an open body posture ready to take in what is spoken. Alert them to using social cues, such as being polite when the other person is talking. You know that it is your turn to speak when you see the other person is done talking.

Activity: The students will think of three questions that they would like to ask a classmate to get to know them better. Brainstorm some questions together such as: What do you want to be when you grow up? What is your favorite movie and why? If you could eat one food for the rest of your life, what would you choose and why? The students will take turns asking and answering the interview questions. Talk with the students about what the process looks like; one person asks the questions, the other person listens and specifically answers the questions. The person asking the question can ask follow-up questions. Invite students to share what they heard and how they got to know their classmate better through communication.

Reflect: Review the interview activity; what did students like or dislike. How can effective communication help improve their daily life?

 **Willpower**

Have students practice polite conversation in pairs as one student reads the Willpower statement as the other listens actively. Then they will switch roles.

Lesson 7

Materials
My Best Me textbook, writing utensils, journal, glass, water

Resources
Student Worksheet: 4yu.info/?i=98407
Parent Summary: 4yu.info/?i=98457

Glossary
personality, survey, chart, unique, analyze, cooperate, efficiently, dominant, intuitive, sociable, critical conscious

Motivation
Students will understand that each of them was born with different personalities and traits. When they learn to discern, accept and appreciate their differences, they will become far more successful at working with others. It is important at this age that students become skilled at recognizing and understanding the innate personality differences in their friends, classmates, family members and even strangers.

Students should come to understand that their strong personality traits are tools with which they have an opportunity to share themselves with those around them. At the same time, they will learn that their weaknesses give others the opportunity to share their strengths or gifts with them. In this process, they learn the value of giving and receiving. In doing so, teams are formed and greatness can be accomplished. In order to successfully work in groups, they will learn to accept others and how to work effectively with personalities that are different from their own. By the end of this lesson, students should understand their dominant personality traits and be more aware of the personalities of others.

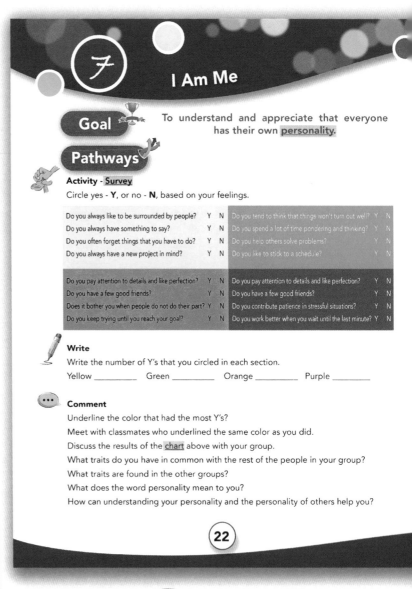

Goal

To learn that there are different personalities and how to discern the differences. Ask them to define "personality"

Pathways

Activity: A fun way to start the lesson is by filling a cup halfway with water. Ask different students to explain to the class how much water is in the cup. Have other students take note of the various ways students express how much water is in the cup. Some may have said that the cup is half full, while others might have described it as half empty. The reason we describe it differently is because of our personality.

Have the students do the survey. Read each of the questions aloud in the four colored areas, then have

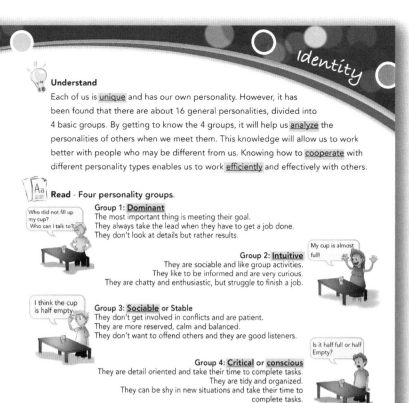

Understand

Each of us is <u>unique</u> and has our own personality. However, it has been found that there are about 16 general personalities, divided into 4 basic groups. By getting to know the 4 groups, it will help us <u>analyze</u> the personalities of others when we meet them. This knowledge will allow us to work better with people who may be different from us. Knowing how to <u>cooperate</u> with different personality types enables us to work <u>efficiently</u> and effectively with others.

Read - Four personality groups.

Group 1: <u>Dominant</u>
The most important thing is meeting their goal.
They always take the lead when they have to get a job done.
They don't look at details but rather results.

Who did not fill up my cup? Who can I talk to?

Group 2: <u>Intuitive</u>
They are sociable and like group activities.
They like to be informed and are very curious.
They are chatty and enthusiastic, but struggle to finish a job.

My cup is almost full!

Group 3: <u>Sociable</u> or Stable
They don't get involved in conflicts and are patient.
They are more reserved, calm and balanced.
They don't want to offend others and they are good listeners.

I think the cup is half empty.

Group 4: <u>Critical</u> or <u>conscious</u>
They are detail oriented and take their time to complete tasks.
They are tidy and organized.
They can be shy in new situations and take their time to complete tasks.

Is it half full or half Empty?

Reflect

After reading the 4 personality groups, which group do I think I am in?
How do I communicate with people who have are in a different personality group?

Willpower

I am aware of my personality, and I recognize and value the personality traits of others.

---

students circle a Y (yes) or N (no) based on their initial gut feeling about the question. Remind them that this is not a test and there are no "correct" answers; they should just circle the answer that feels right to them. After they have finished filling out the questions, the students will count and record how many "Y's" they circled in each of the colored areas.

Comment: If two areas had the same amount of "Y's", they can circle them both and choose whichever color they would like. The students will then be instructed to go sit with their classmates that had the same color circled as themselves. Once the students have been separated into the four groups, they will discuss the questions in this section of the workbook. The goal is for the students to notice how they behave, answer the questions and interact among each other; probably in a very similar way. Have them also take note of the students in the other groups and how they behave. After the groups have had enough time to discuss, engage in a whole class discussion.

As the teacher, observe the behavior of each group and write down a few characteristics. At the end of the activity, ask each group to assign a representative to give a short recap on what happened in the group. Then ask students what they observed in the behavior of the four groups. One group might have been loud and boisterous, another group might have been quiet, sitting around looking at each other, while a third group might have completed the talk promptly and moved on to other activities, etc. Remember, we are analyzing personality groups and their dominant behaviors. Maintain a safe, non-judgmental atmosphere where everyone feels validated.

Understand/Read: Go through this section of the workbook together. Talk about the pictures of the cups of water and how four different people saw the same situation in four very different ways (relate back to this same activity if you chose to do it with the class at the beginning.)

Discuss with the class how unique each individual person is. Even when we have the same end goal, people with different personalities pursue different paths to meet the goal. It is important that we are aware of our dominant personality traits as well as the traits of others when working as a group. When we have more insight into ourselves and others, we are more likely to complete a task efficiently and effectively, and be in harmony with others.

Reflect: Make sure the students understand that within the small classroom, there are many different traits represented and that the traits described are just a few. Have each group work together to try and guess which color describes the group's dominant personality traits.

Willpower

Have each color group read the Willpower statement aloud together, one group at a time.

Lesson 8

Materials
My Best Me textbook, writing utensils, paper for an acrostic poem, puzzle pieces—these can be made from cutting construction paper into different shapes that can be put back together. Be sure to add a piece for yourself; you are part of the classroom life and image, a wide assortment of art supplies.

* Suggestion: A great book to read to continue the conversation about being unique is *A Bad Case of the Stripes* by David Shannon.

Resources
Student Worksheet: 4yu.info/?i=98408
Parent Summary: 4yu.info/?i=98458

Glossary
masterpiece, irreplaceable, acrostic

Motivation
It is valuable for the students' confidence and manner of operating to have clear insight into how unique they are. Students will come to understand that they are who they are for a special reason, to accomplish a particular destiny. Students have already discovered how they are different from others and these differences can sometimes lead to insecurities that are exploited by advertising and even social media.

In order to help students be comfortable in their own skin, it is essential that they learn to embrace their individuality with all its different traits and characteristics. It is okay to admire something about someone else, but it is important to be content within ourselves; with who we are. Students should find value in their uniqueness.

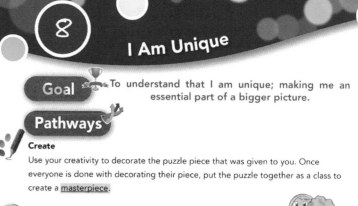

8   I Am Unique

Goal To understand that I am unique; making me an essential part of a bigger picture.

Pathways

Create
Use your creativity to decorate the puzzle piece that was given to you. Once everyone is done with decorating their piece, put the puzzle together as a class to create a masterpiece.

Comment
Did any of the puzzle pieces look the same?
How did you know where your puzzle piece belonged?
What would happen if one of the pieces was missing or lost?
How did you feel once the whole puzzle was complete?

Understand
Life is like a series of different puzzles in which people are the pieces that fit together to complete the image. Each person is a unique piece; irreplaceable and necessary for the success of the whole puzzle.

 Your value is measured by the simple fact of your uniqueness, not by your possessions or appearance. It is impossible to duplicate who you are. Think about all of the ways that you are different from the people around you. We are all unique in the way that we think, speak, act, feel and look. Our individual personalities also help make each of us different and interesting. Some

---

Goal

Students will have the opportunity to reflect on their own characteristics that make them who they are and a unique part of the big picture, wherever they are

Pathways

Create: Give each student a puzzle piece that you cut out ahead of time. Have students write their name on the back side of their puzzle piece. Give them the opportunity to color or decorate their puzzle piece however they choose. Supply them with a great variety of art supplies. Stimulate them to do something exceptional with their puzzle piece—an expression of who they are. Once the students are done designing their piece, allow the pieces to dry. Let them work together to construct the puzzle. Students should be

people are shy, while others are outgoing. In addition, we all have different passions, abilities and talents. Some people are very athletic, while others are artistic. Think about how boring it would be if every person were exactly the same! Without each individual, our world would not be complete.

Write

Write your name vertically along the side, from top to bottom. Next to each letter, create an acrostic poem by writing a special characteristic or fact about yourself that starts with each letter of your name.

Reflect

How did I decide what to write for each letter?
Did I write the same characteristics as anyone else in the classroom?
How do I differ from my classmates?

I am special because I

Willpower

I am the only me the world will ever see.

25

traits fitting together in different images and manners to make a world that is whole. Have the students think about what the classroom would be like if every single person had the same personality traits. What if everyone looked the same, dressed the same, liked the same things, and acted exactly the same? Would your classroom be exciting or boring? The students should see that having unique personalities and qualities makes the classroom, and life, more fun and exciting. We are always learning and growing from the people around us.

Write: Students will write an acrostic poem about themselves, allowing them to reflect on their own individual character traits that make them special. Before having the students begin, show them an example of an acrostic poem (or make one together using your own name). Once the students understand what an acrostic poem is, they will create one in the workbook with their own name. They will need to write their name vertically on the left side of the paper. Then, they will write one word or phrase using each letter that describes one of their unique character traits. Once these are finished, they can share with a partner or the whole class.

Reflect: The students will end the lesson by writing one of the qualities that makes them unique. This can be something silly, like in the suggested reading book; the girl is unique because she loves lima beans. It can be something interesting about the way they look, or it could be a unique skill or ability that they have. The students can share these qualities to learn something new and fun about each of their classmates.

aware that all of the pieces are needed to make the image complete, yet each piece is uniquely different and beautiful, adding to the whole impression.

Comment: After the students have constructed the puzzle and taped it together, hang it up for everyone to admire and discuss. The distinct shapes and decorations, convey different messages, yet they fit together tightly and create a very unique image that cannot be replicated by other classes. Talk about what the puzzle would look like if a piece were lost. Without all of the pieces, the puzzle along with its image would be incomplete.

Understand: Read this section aloud or have the students read it quietly in pairs. Ask the students to explain in their own words how life is like a series of different puzzles. When we are able to explain something, we are able to truly understand it. Students should realize that all the different pieces of a puzzle are needed to make it complete. Puzzles can be compared to groups of people with every one of our unique personalities and

Willpower

Have the students read the Willpower statement aloud together and then everyone will say a unique quality that they have aloud.

Lesson 9

Materials
My Best Me textbook, writing utensils, paper
* Suggestion: a good book to introduce this lesson with is *Hygiene ...You Stink* by Julia Cook.

Resources
Student Worksheet: 4yu.info/?i=98409
Parent Summary: 4yu.info/?i=98459

Glossary
hygiene, contrast, odors, toxins, moist, eliminate, attractive, confidence, convince, offensive

Motivation

Here's the truth: the way we look and smell influence how others perceive us. As children mature and become adolescents, their bodies begin to grow and change, requiring them to adapt their hygiene. It is important that students become more aware of their hygiene and learn how to take care of themselves effectively without being told to do so. A large part of caring for ourselves is making sure our body is clean and presentable. At this age, most students will already be responsible for their personal hygiene. Their parents might not be reminding them any longer to brush their teeth or wash with soap. Most of your students are probably taking their bath or shower alone, without their parents' help.

It is now the student's responsibility to make sure their bodies and clothes are properly cared for and cleaned. As their bodies change, they most likely will start to produce odors that they did not have before. It's important that they become aware of this so they can take the appropriate steps to avoid discomfort or embarrassment for themselves, as well as others.

Students should clearly understand how their appearance, odors and presentation influence other people around them from the very first moment of any encounter.

9   I Take Care of My Body

Goal
To learn the importance of proper hygiene

Pathways

Observe
With a partner, write under each picture how often you do each action, what product you use to do each action, and explain the reason for your choice to your partner.

Comment
Why is it important to be clean?
Do you notice when you need to clean yourself? How?
Do you feel different when you are clean in  contrast to when you are dirty? How?

Understand
Humans produce different body odors. The body odors that we produce as we start to get older can be clearly noticed in our sweat. Sweat contains "toxins" and hormones that are produced in parts of our bodies that are moist. When these toxins

Goal

Students will understand how proper hygiene practices will promote good health, being comfortable and finding favor with others around them

Pathways

Observe: The students will look at each of the pictures and fill in the blanks with how often they do each of the activities. Give them the freedom to add any other hygiene-related activities they practice that are not mentioned (e.g., changing clothes, cleaning their nose, using deodorant, flossing their teeth). The objective of this activity is for students to reflect on their current hygiene routines and maybe even learn from one another. Be sure they understand the meaning of "hygiene."

After giving students time to answer each question,

are present, they smell bad. Fortunately, the solution is simple! Keeping our bodies clean and drinking plenty of water are basics actions to take in order to <u>eliminate</u> the bad odors we can have. Maintaining a clean body is called hygiene and it includes washing our hands after we use the bathroom, taking a bath or shower every day, and brushing our teeth after we eat. When our bodies are clean, our smell is pleasant, and we wear fresh clothes, our presence is <u>attractive</u> to others. It also makes us feel better about ourselves emotionally and mentally. Cleanliness supports our <u>confidence</u>!

 Write

Adam is a student just like you, but does not like to bathe. Write a friendly letter to <u>convince</u> him to clean himself every day. Be kind as you explain why, and then how, to do this. Choose your words carefully, because you do not want to be <u>offensive</u> or hurt his feelings.

Dear Adam,

 Reflect

What was easy about writing this letter to Adam?
What was difficult about writing this letter to Adam?
What made it difficult to write the letter?
Why is it important that we have good hygiene?

Willpower

I use proper hygiene to be healthy and confident.

---

discuss each picture. You can make a class graph where students can mark how often they do each activity (only include students who feel comfortable sharing). Then have a class discussion about hygiene routines, such as washing our hands before we eat, when we come inside and after using the restroom to keep from spreading germs. On the other hand, our whole body only needs to be cleaned once a day. What is involved with healthy dental care? Should we change socks every day as well as underwear? What are some big challenges in being consistent with hygiene habits?

Comment: This is a sensitive subject for 4th graders because of the insecurities they might experience due to the changes in their bodies. Guide the students in a conversation about hygiene using the comment questions in the workbook. They can brainstorm reasons why cleanliness is important. Students should understand the consequences of improper hygiene: sickness, infecting others, discomfort, rejection, and awkwardness.

Understand: Be aware of students who have difficulty with their hygiene. Explain that as bodies change, we start to produce odors because of hormones. Hormones are chemical substances our bodies make that act like messengers, and control how different cells and organs in the body work. Talk about how to maintain cleanliness and what that looks like. Be cognizant of family challenges or living conditions that might hinder them from doing this.

Write: Students will write a letter to an imaginary classmate named Adam who needs some advice on hygiene (please change the name if you have an Adam in the class). Help students to understand that hygiene can involve factors that might be out of the student's control (e.g., a sick mom at home, struggling with means to purchase necessary hygiene items, unstable living arrangement, etc.). When students write these letters, they should address the topic with respect and sensitivity. Have them imagine how they might feel if someone told them that they did not smell nice or looked grimy. It might hurt their feelings or embarrass them. The goal is for the students to convince Adam of the value of taking care of himself, and explaining the ways to do that. Of course they can offer Adam their help and assistance in the letter they write.

Reflect: Once the letters are written, they can share them with the class. Discuss different ways of addressing sensitive topics like this one without hurting anyone's feelings. Remind them that this is just like being in our classroom; we have to be respectful when talking with our friends about sensitive issues (whether about hygiene or another topic).

Willpower

Ask each student for a 1 - 2 word answer to the question, "why hygiene is important?" Once everyone has answered, have everyone read the Willpower statement aloud together.

Lesson 10

Materials
My Best Me textbook, writing utensils, paper, audiovisual equipment

Resources
Student Worksheet: 4yu.info/?i=98410
Parent Summary: 4yu.info/?i=98460
Video: 4yu.info/?i=94091

Glossary
affects, optimistic, undesirable, constructive, perspective, whiny, inevitable, cope, Fixed Mindset, intimidating, approach

Motivation
Our attitude affects the outcome of every situation in our life. We can choose to look for the positive in each day and in every challenging situation, or dwell on the negative. Students are going to be faced with disappointments and hardships; setbacks are a part of life. It is important that they learn ways of coping with undesirable situations. They also need to realize that the choice is always theirs to be made: to be optimistic and look for the best in every situation, or to be negative and complain about it (or just give up).

When students learn the power of being positive, they will discover that they are more pleasant to be around, more creative and happier. Be creative and demonstrate how unpleasant it is to be around people who are critical, negative or complaining. Teach students to use constructive and affirmative words to help them navigate undesirable situations. It will change the direction of what is happening with and to them. They need to understand that they make that choice.

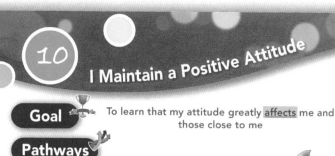

I Maintain a Positive Attitude

Goal To learn that my attitude greatly affects me and those close to me

Pathways

Write
Have you ever heard the saying, "When life gives you lemons, make lemonade"? What does this saying mean to you?
_____

Observe
Our attitude in or about a situation greatly affects the outcome of that situation. We pick our attitude with our words. Positive and optimistic words create positive attitudes, which help us deal with undesirable situations and get better results than negative words and attitudes. Write constructive words these students below can use to cope with each situation.

Comment
Do you think positive and optimistic words can affect the outcome of each situation?
How would a negative attitude affect the situation?
How do you use words (positive or negative) in your own life?

30

Goal

The students will learn why and how to use constructive and productive words to maintain a positive outlook on life

Pathways

Write: Once the students have answered the question about the meaning of the saying, ask them for examples of making lemonade from lemons. Talk about changing something undesirable into something positive and worthwhile.

Observe: Ask students for examples of a positive attitude and a negative attitude. Ask someone to share an example of both from their life. We can choose how we will react to disappointment and unwelcome situations. We can chose to mope and complain, or look

Video:
How can perspective
change your attitude?
4yu.info/?i=94091

4yu.info/?i=94091

Understand
Our attitude directly affects how others see us. When we are happy and positive, others like to be around us. When we are negative, angry and whiny, others do not want to be around us. Life will not always go as planned, and disappointments are inevitable. One way to cope with disappointment is to maintain an optimistic view and positive attitude, no matter what. Imagine that you study for a math test, but still get a low grade. You feel disappointed, naturally, but you can choose a fixed mindset, which believes you will never learn, or you can choose a growth mindset by believing you can always learn more about something, even math. Choosing the positive attitude or mindset produces peace and happiness.

Activity
Think about something that is difficult and challenging for you. How can you change your mindset or attitude to make the situation better or less intimidating? Are there positive and constructive words you can use to change the situation? Can you change your actions and approach to make it better? Write your plan down in a journal.

Reflect
I am given the chance each day to make it powerful and great—the choice is mine. My attitude determines how my day will turn out. What can I change for a better outcome?

Willpower

I find happiness each day by making a conscious decision to have a positive attitude, no matter what.

31

---

for opportunities and the positive in situations. A positive and optimistic attitude starts with being kind toward ourselves and then to others: students need to know that they are stronger than they think; they can learn from every difficult situation, and that growth develops perseverance.

As the students will look at the pictures, direct them to use positive words to help self-talk each individual through their situation. Encourage them to think creatively and allow them to share before you give them ideas.

Comment: Invite the students to share the positive words they decided to use in each picture. Discuss how having a negative attitude would affect each of these situations.

Understand: How we handle disappointment affects our overall happiness and how others view us. Have the students think about the people that they like to be around. Are they people who are happy, fun and friendly, or are they moody, miserable and complaining?

Optimistic people maintain a positive attitude, change their behavior to make situations more favorable and use uplifting and constructive words for themselves and others.

Remind students that it is okay to feel sad or disappointed. These are natural feelings that we have and need to work through at times. However, to let sadness, disappointment and hardship define us and our situations will greatly affect us in negative ways. Each person has a choice regarding the attitude they take and the words and actions resulting from it. Positive doesn't mean pretending everything is okay when it's not; that's denial. It means making the best of every situation, even difficult ones.

Activity: The students will think of something that is challenging for them (i.e., something that they are not good at, or they don't like doing). For example, math; if you always have a negative attitude about it, you block your ability to use your creative, problem-solving mindset and can-do attitude to face the challenge and press through. Student's will write a plan on how they can improve their attitude or change their actions to conquer an undesirable task or situation. Have them share their ideas with others to contribute encouragement and inspiration. You can even develop this into a classroom trait, where students mentor and encourage one another to always look for the silver lining around the dark cloud.

Reflect: Have students reflect on their own attitudes. Do they tend to look for the positive in situations or do they tend to look for the negative?

Willpower

With a partner, students should practice a positive attitude by responding to a negative statement with positive words. After everyone has practiced, repeat the Willpower statement aloud together.

Lesson 11

Materials
My Best Me textbook, writing utensils, paper, audiovisual equipment

Resources
Student Worksheet: 4yu.info/?i=98411
Parent Summary: 4yu.info/?i=98461
Video: "Learnstorm Growth Mindset: The Truth About Your Brain" - 4yu.info/?i=94101

Glossary
intelligence, complex, potential, programmed, assumption, gymnastics, cement, putty, stretch

Motivation
The brain is an amazing organ. Though scientists have been studying it ardently for hundreds of years, and neuroscience has made significant discoveries, the brain is still an unexplored universe of possibilities. If your students can walk away from this lesson with just one truth, it should be that the brain is flexible or "elastic." If students put their mind to something, they can achieve it.

The problem has been that our society assumed that the brain is a fixed entity; that our talents, gifts, and intelligence are "set in stone," and that there's nothing we can do to change that, but that is false. We will see in this lesson that scientists are proving that the brain can adapt, grow and change. This is the difference between a Growth Mindset and a Fixed Mindset.

Having a Growth Mindset also indicates that you take full responsibility for the things you learn or do not learn in life. It is your brain, your mindset and your application of hope that helps you become successful.

---

11 — Elastic Brain!

Goal
To understand that my abilities, intelligence and talents are not limited, because my brain can grow

Pathways

Video: 4yu.info/?i=94101
Watch this clip:

4yu.info/?i=94101

Understand
Our head brain is the most complex organ in our bodies. Every year, science and education make new, amazing discoveries about the power and potential of the brain. For many years, most scientists thought that a person was born with a certain amount of intelligence and ability; that the brain was "fixed" or "programmed" and could not be changed. More than 30 years ago, Dr. Carol Dweck decided to challenge that assumption, believing that the brain actually can grow in its abilities, and that we can improve our intelligence. Dr. Dweck's discovery has changed how we think about our brains. Dr. Dweck calls it Growth Mindset vs. Fixed Mindset.

 Read
Our brains are actually like the stretchy, sticky jelly hands; able to stretch and do things we might have thought impossible. In a Fixed Mindset we tell ourselves that we **can't** become better at something, such as math. With a Growth Mindset, the opposite is true. We tell ourselves that we **can** grow and get better, which causes our brain to get on the move and make it happen. Just like the stretchy, sticky hand, our brain has the potential to stretch and expand and reach further! This is called the Power of Yet; we may not yet be great in gymnastics, but we can and will improve and get better! It's like we stretch and twist our brains to think in different ways. If one way doesn't work to solve a math problem, then we try another way until we get it right. Our brains are not like cement that cannot be formed into

32

Goal

A Growth Mindset (or outlook) will help students own their learning process in every area of life; maximizing their brain as a powerful tool for reaching their goals

Pathways

Video: Watch the video. What is the difference between a Growth Mindset and a Fixed Mindset?

Understand: Help your 4th graders grasp the concept that their brain is stretchy and able to grow and develop beyond what was thought for many years. You will set your students up for a paradigm shift in their thinking! Here's the truth: the brain is unlimited. We are not destined to be weak in math, science or reading (or any other subject) for the rest of our lives. The key is having a genuine desire to learn. With that

something else once it has dried. Our brains are like Silly <u>Putty;</u> elastic and stretchy! Just like in the "Learnstorm" video above, your brain is like a muscle. The more you exercise your brain, the stronger and smarter it gets! You need to continue to exercise your brain to keep it strong and smart.

Write

1. What is a talent or ability you want to be more like the stretchy, sticky hand?
_____

2. What step(s) can you take to become more "elastic" in this area?
_____

Game - The Yet Game

Challenge: change your brain by changing your words. Change the Fixed Mindset sentence on the left into Growth Mindset sentences on the right

Fixed Mindset Words	Growth Mindset Words
I can't do that!	_____
I don't know how to do that.	_____
I tried!	_____
That is too hard for me to do!	_____
That is impossible!	_____
I am scared that I will fail.	_____

Reflect

Have you ever used Fixed Mindset words? Why?
Was it difficult to change the Fixed Mindset Words into Growth Mindset words? Why?
Can you explain why the Growth Mindset words are powerful and promising?

MINDSET IS EVERYTHING

Willpower

I will <u>stretch</u> my brain because it is a powerful tool for achieving any goals I set.

33

---

desire and applying ourselves with consistency, we can improve in any area. Does it mean that if we are terrible at basketball, we will be the next NBA superstar? No. But we will get better! Help your students understand that their brain can take them further than they ever thought possible! It all has to do with their desire!

Read: Our brains are actually like the stretchy, sticky, jelly hand toy. With a Growth Mindset, we tell ourselves that we can grow and get better at something, so that causes our brain to stretch, expand and reach things we thought were impossible.

When we do not exercise and stretch our muscles and joints, they become stiff, slow and limited. That can happen to our brain. We need to keep it agile by continuously exercising it by learning, assigning it tasks and stretching it as much as we can.

Talk through the concept of "The Power of Yet" with your class. They may not "yet" be good at the hula hoop, but with practice, they will be. Ask students to share one "yet" goal with the class. For example, "I am not yet

---

great at playing the guitar, but I will practice until I am." Make sure this is voluntary and avoid pressing this too much.

After this exercise, reassure your students that if one way doesn't work to solve a math problem (or another area of presumed weakness), then we try another way until we get it right. Our brains are not like cement that cannot be formed into something else once it has dried. Our brains are like elastic; stretchy and flexible!

Activity: The students should change the Fixed Mindset phrases to Growth Mindset phrases by adding the word, "yet." Allow students to share their Growth Mindset statements and write some of these down on construction paper for future use in your classroom. Let your students know that the only mindset that works in your classroom is the Growth Mindset. Encourage students to correct each other and use phrases that support the Growth Mindset.

Reflect: Ask the students to write down a few Fixed Mindset phrases they have used in the past. Then have them rip up the paper, destroying those phrases, putting them in the garbage where they belong. Have everyone say, "I have a Growth Mindset. I can do anything I set my mind to do."

Willpower

Challenge your students to stretch their brain every day with a new fact. Suggest keeping a diary of daily acquired new information; training themselves to expect increased knowledge and ability in any area they choose.

Lesson 12

Materials
My Best Me textbook, writing utensils, paper, audiovisual equipment

Resources
Student Worksheet: 4yu.info/?i=98412
Parent Summary: 4yu.info/?i=98462
Videos: Nutrition Guide - 4yu.info/?i=94111

Glossary
recognize, fertilizer, consume, preservatives, food coloring, caffeine, saturated fats, processed, refined, manufactured, diet, proportions, proteins, consider

Motivation
To evaluate our overall health, we should consider our consumption patterns. Many of us eat greater portions than we need of foods that require little preparation and are saturated with chemicals. One of the first steps to positive physical change is to understand the direct correlation between the foods we choose to put into our bodies and our overall health.

Each day we face the decision of what we should put into our bodies. Wholesome, unprocessed foods can help us stay healthy and energetic, and will allow us to grow strong. Unhealthy foods are typically processed or manufactured, and generally contain preservatives, food coloring, saturated fats, sugar or caffeine, and can harm our bodies. Often, the quick and easy packaged foods that many children eat for snacks are unhealthy options.

It is important for students to become more aware of their food choices and the effects they can have on their health. It is good to teach students balance, starting at a young age. They should realize they do not have to completely cut certain kinds of foods out of their diet, but work toward a balance of food groups that ensures they get all of the nutrients they need.

12 — Eat Healthy, Grow Healthy

Goal
To learn to recognize the foods that help me grow healthy and strong

Pathways

Read

Martin is learning how to grow plants. He knows that plants require water, light, fresh soft soil and removing weeds from the area. Martin also knows that fertilizer contains nutrients that help plants grow stronger and faster.

One day, Martin decided to try to quicken the growing process by using more fertilizer on the soil than advised. He thought, "If a little bit is good, more will be better". After a few days, Martin was surprised at the results the fertilizer had on his plants.

Comment
Why did Martin's plant suffer and die?
What could Martin have done to avoid this?
What advice would you give to Martin?

Understand
We often consume more food than we need to be healthy. This decision can cause us problems in our bodies. Therefore, learning about food and how it nourishes our bodies is key to an active and energetic life. The foods we eat have different nutritional values and we must understand the effect our food choices have on our bodies to make the

Goal

Students will learn the importance of having a balanced and healthy diet. They will analyze their current eating habits and design a balanced eating planv

Pathways

Read: Read the story of Martin together as a class. Discuss whether Martin is making the right choice by adding the extra nutrients to his plant.

Comment: Use the questions to talk about what happened to Martin's plant, and to lead into a discussion about balance. Excess, can do more harm than good. That is why balance in all aspects of our life is so important, but especially in our diet. By partaking in a wide variety of foods, it will ensure that we get everything we need in the areas of energy, growth, vitality and

best choices. Some foods contain <u>preservatives</u>, <u>food coloring</u>, <u>caffeine</u>, sugar, or <u>saturated fats</u>, which can have negative effects on our well-being. There are also raw, unprocessed and natural foods that are better choices than the <u>processed</u>, <u>refined</u> or <u>manufactured</u> foods. As we learn about the differences in our food choices, we will make better selections and eat to maintain a healthy lifestyle.

Another way to bring balance to our <u>diet</u> is to consume foods from the different food groups in the recommended <u>proportions</u>. There are six general categories: vegetables, fruits, <u>proteins</u>, grains, dairy and oils. Using these groups as our guide for food selection, we can ensure that our bodies are getting all of the nutrients we need to grow and flourish.

 Activity

Draw a balanced meal plan for a day. Think about the food groups that were mentioned above as you plan your meals.

BREAKFAST	SNACK	LUNCH	SNACK	DINNER

 Reflect

What did I have to <u>consider</u> when planning my meals?
Why can it be difficult at times to decide what is healthy to eat?
In my daily life, do I choose to nourish myself in a healthy way?
Whose responsibility is it to be mindful of my diet? Mine? My parents? Why?

Willpower

I choose to eat healthy foods in balanced proportions to ensure my body is healthy and strong.

35

---

overall well-being.

An extension and aide to this conversation might be to look at the MyPlate model. MyPlate is a guide that helps us create a diet that is balanced and full of nutrients for our bodies (there are others websites as well). This is an excellent visual tool that can help us determine how much we should be eating from each of the food groups. Use this video to help the students understand. 4yu.info/?i=94111

Understand: Read this together as a class, to start the process of discovering and maintaining a healthy balance. Talk with your students about what foods would belong in each of the five or six food groups. You can make a chart on the board. Ask students why they think sugar is not added as one of the groups. Information and training, allows students to discover how and why to take care of themselves and in the end, they will want to make the right choices for themselves.

Our body needs a great variety of nutrients to be able to function correctly. Help your students understand

---

that moderation and balance are key, and nourishing ourselves with variety is a great way to create a healthy and balanced diet. As a concrete example, you might point out that having dessert now and then is fine, as long as they aren't living on a diet of sugar and candy!

Activity: Students will draw a balanced meal plan based on what they have learned. You can have students work this from two sides. First, what does their food consumption look like? Have them write down all the foods and drinks they consume in one day. Second, in contrast, have students write down what they would eat for meals and snacks if they were to pursue a balanced and healthy diet. Prompt the students to keep the MyPlate guide in mind, but also to make their plans realistic. When the students are done, allow them to share their work, ideas and thoughts.

Reflect: Discuss the process of choosing foods, and have your students share how they felt about the process. It is difficult to make healthy food choices every day because, often, unhealthy foods are tasty, easy, quick, and readily available. Encourage students to invite their family to work together to make healthy eating choices. Sometimes the impact is greater by just making one small change at a time. For example, maybe they can begin by challenging themselves to eat one piece of fruit and one vegetable serving each day.

Willpower

Have each student write down one healthy food they will add to their diet before everyone reads the Willpower statement aloud together.

Lesson 13

Materials
My Best Me textbook, writing utensils, paper, ball for kickball or other activity

Resources
Student Worksheet: 4yu.info/?i=98413
Parent Summary: 4yu.info/?i=98463

Glossary
foster, promotes, calories, discharge, invigorates, caution, judge, harshly, modest, recommended, commitment

Motivation
Help your students understand the great benefits that daily exercise has on their body. Exercise helps:
• increase levels of happiness
• build muscles and strengthen bones
• maintain flexibility
• reduce the risk of disease
• stimulate brain activity and memory
• improve sleep
• reduce pain
• achieve weight loss and maintenance
• increase energy levels
• eliminate toxins
• improve skin conditions
• reduce stress and tension
• improve performance
• teach goal setting

With the increasing use of technology and video games, it can become difficult for kids to get out and exercise. Help students discover the importance of making time every day for some physical activity. It is recommended that we have physical activity for at least thirty minutes daily. Being active is good for our body, mind and soul.

Physical activity can be walking a dog in the neighborhood, walking up the stairs, shopping, taking a bike ride, stretching, dancing, etc. Being in movement instead of sitting or laying down is very important for children and teenagers.

13 Exercise!

Goal To learn why exercising benefits my body

Pathways

Activity: Let's Move

Warm-up Exercise Cool Down

 Comment
Why should we stretch before physical activity?
Do you like physical activity? Please explain.
How do you feel physically after you have exercised? Emotionally? Mentally?
What type of physical activity is your favorite?

Understand
When we exercise, our bodies produce chemical substances called hormones that make us grow, help us stay emotionally stable, and <u>foster</u> our health and strength. Exercising also <u>promotes</u> the burning of <u>calories</u> and fat, and the <u>discharge</u> of toxins. This combination helps us stay fit and energetic. When we exercise, it activates our brain and <u>invigorates</u> us to face the tasks and responsibilities of life.

To experience all the benefits above, it is recommended that we exercise for at least 30 minutes every day. Some examples of exercise are: running, biking, walking, playing sports, swimming, and dancing. If we make exercise fun and look for something we enjoy, we will continue with being physically active.

36

Goal

The students will be motivated to engage in exercise on a daily basis as well as reflect on how often they are physically active during their days

Pathways

Activity: Plan an exercise activity with your class. It can be jumping jacks, dancing, running, doing burpees, etc. This will engage students in somewhat intense physical activity to get them thinking about exercise. Lead the class in a warm up activity. Explain the importance of warming up in preparation for exercise. It increases circulation which loosens the joints, increases the blood flow to the muscles and helps prevent injuries.

Next, decide on a game or exercise for the students to play that will keep them physically active. You can come up with the game beforehand, or the students can vote

A note of caution: While exercise is vital for our physical, emotional, and mental health, be careful not to judge yourself too harshly if your exercise level is modest, especially at first. Start small! We all do.

Write

Do you exercise for 30 minutes every day?

Make a list of the physical activities and the amount of time that you exercise each day.

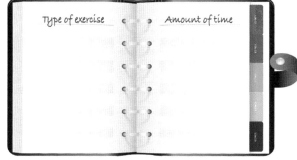

Type of exercise	Amount of time

Are there any improvements that you can make?

Write an exercise goal for yourself. I will ... and steps to how you will achieve your goal.

_____

_____

_____

Reflect

Do I engage in the recommended amount of exercise each day?

What obstacles keep me from exercising each day?

How can I overcome these obstacles and be more active?

Willpower

I make a commitment to exercise each day to enjoy health in my body, mind and emotions.

37

---

on their favorite game (e.g., kickball, dodge ball, soccer, relay races, obstacle course, etc.). Make sure the activity causes their heart rate to go up!

After the activity, give students the opportunity to drink some water and cool down, maybe even doing some simple stretches to allow an abundant blood flow into the used muscles. Again, talk about the importance of staying hydrated and cooling down after physical activity. Suggestion: You might want to do this lesson at the end of the day if students can't change clothes or freshen up after the event.

Comment: Use these common questions to talk about the activity. Remind the students that they are engaging in a physical activity any time their heart rate increases and they are using their muscles. Sometimes we do not even realize that we are exercising when we are having fun. Share experiences with physical activity; how exercising makes them feel, both during and after. We might feel tired or out of breath while we exercise, but accomplished and energetic after we are done.

Understand: After reading, make a list as a class of all of the benefits that exercise has on our whole being. The students should be able to put into words how important it is for them to take the time out of their day for some physical activity.

Write: The students will make a list of the physical activities they engage in each day. Remind them that this can be at recess, in PE, or outside of school. Next to each activity, they will write the actual amount of time they spend on that activity. Then the students will analyze if they are spending enough time on exercise each day. Based on their finding, the students will set a goal to either do more physical activity, or think about how they can enhance what they are already doing.

You can encourage increased physical activity during recess by teaching your students the games you played when you were at school: jump rope, elastics, hopscotch, hula hoops, etc. If your school does not already have a "no technology during free time" policy, consider discussing putting this into place with school administration. The time when students arrive to school, have recess/free time, or wait for their bus or pick up at the end of the day is a great opportunity for them to engage in physical activity or to socialize. It will change your students' behavior and learning processes for the better.

Reflect: Help students evaluate their physical activity. Sometimes small changes can make big impacts, such as taking the stairs instead of the elevator, or doing something together with a friend.

Willpower

Explain what it means to make a commitment. Have students read the Willpower statement aloud together.

Lesson 14

Materials
My Best Me textbook, writing utensils, paper

Resources
Student Worksheet: 4yu.info/?i=98414
Parent Summary: 4yu.info/?i=98464

Glossary
stressful, credit, skill, uncomfortable, scenarios, comfortable

Motivation
Students at this age will begin to make choices based upon their peers. They start to notice what others around them are doing and might feel pressured to fit in and avoid conflict. Sometimes fitting in means making choices that are unwise, immoral or dangerous because of peer pressure.

This is the age for students to learn the value of using their voice and to feel comfortable saying "no." This will require them to understand the emotions, feelings and turmoil inside of them when faced with situations in which they should speak out.

Students should realize it is not always easy to say "no," but it is vitally important that they follow their inner gut feelings and feel equipped to take a stand. We need to encourage them to make the right choice, and be willing to voice their decision, even if it may not be the popular one or might hurt some feelings. In the end, it takes more courage to say "no" than it does to follow or join in on something that they know is wrong.

14   I Stand Up

Goal   To learn how to calmly avoid or handle stressful situations

Pathways

Read
Jaime is a hard-working student who spends a lot of time every night completing his homework. His friend, Robert, does not like to do his homework. Instead, he spends a lot of time playing video games.

On the bus, Robert asks Jaime if he can copy his homework so he can get credit for completing it on time.

How would you advise Jaime to handle the situation? _____
_____
_____

Understand
Like Jaime, we will often be faced with situations where we want to say "no," but say "yes." Being able to say "no" to our peers without feeling bad is not easy to do, but it is an important skill to develop.

We should never make decisions because we are afraid of being rejected or embarrassed. It is often easier to say "yes" just to avoid negative feelings, but we must remain true to ourselves and always respond in honesty. It is helpful to understand why we feel the way we do when we say "no." Sometimes doing the right thing can "feel" like it's wrong. We must be honest with ourselves and become comfortable saying "no" when necessary.

Goal

Students will discover that taking a stand is not always easy. They will practice different ways of saying "no" in a friendly yet firm manner, using life scenarios

Pathways

Read: When students are done reading the story of Jaime, they will use their best judgment to advise him on how to handle the situation. It is tricky because his friend might get angry. However, "no" is the right choice.
• Jaime is helping his friend by saying "no." It will require his friend to do the assigned tasks the next time, and truly prepare himself for his future.
• It is not fair; Jaime worked hard while the other boy played video games.
• It is unethical to copy someone's work and turn it in as our own.

Even if we become very skilled at saying "no", there will be times when we will still feel <u>uncomfortable</u> responding that way. That's because it takes courage to do the best thing. Sometimes doing and saying the healthy thing will be difficult, but it will always be beneficial in the end. Remember to follow your gut feeling.

Activity - Role Play

Read the following <u>scenarios</u>. Act out each situation with a partner using the word "no" in a firm but kind manner.

- Your friends want to come over to your house after school to play, but you have a book report due the next day that is not finished.
- You and a friend find a cell phone that was left on the bus. Your friend tells you to put in into your backpack to keep it, since you found it.
- Your little brother bought a new game that you promised to play with him. Friends stop by and invite you to hang out.
- Your friends that you sit with at lunch are making fun of another student that is sitting by himself. Your friends ask you to join in.

Reflect

Do I use the word "no" when necessary?

What are some different ways I can say "no"?

How do I feel when I say "no"? Why do I feel that way?

How can I say no in a way that doesn't make me feel guilty or wrong?

Willpower

I am <u>comfortable</u> using the word "no" for the well-being of others, as well as for my own peace of mind.

Comment: Survey the students to see who would have said "yes" and shared their homework, and who would have said "no." Have both groups defend why they made their choice to discover the motivation of their hearts. Next, have the students share situations in which they might have to say "no" to a peer. Encourage students to share how it feels to say "no" to someone, the feelings it causes and why. Does it make them uncomfortable or scared? Are they confident saying "no?"

Understand: Read this section together. The students will brainstorm ways they can say "no" when a situation or request makes them uncomfortable. We have to make choices; some are easy while others can be very difficult. In many situations, we have just seconds to make our choice while sometimes, we have more time to ponder. Either way, the decisions we make will impact our life either positively or negatively. It is important to understand our feelings and know our personal convictions, so we can make the best choice

for ourselves, even when the pressure is on. Encourage students to listen to and heed their inner voice; it is usually a soft, nudging alert. The best way to get better at saying "no" is to practice.

Make a class chart of different ways to say "no." Some examples, might include:
• Say no and give a reason why • Leave without saying anything • Say "no" and that you will talk about this another time • Ask questions to get insight • Say you want to think about it, and you will get back with them • Do not argue • Give no reaction • Say "no" firmly • Give a better suggestion

Your class can add more suggestions on how they might say "no."

Activity: The students will practice using different strategies to say "no" by acting out the scenarios in the workbook. Feel free to add any other scenarios relevant and appropriate for your class and school. The students can break off into small groups to practice first, or volunteers can come up and act out the scenarios in front of the class. In each of the scenarios, saying "no" is the best choice that can be made. Have the students talk about why it can be hard to say "no." It takes courage to make the right choice. Encourage the students to share positive situations when they were able to say "no."

Reflect: Take the opportunity to motivate your students to take someone's "no" for what it is. As much as they need to learn to say "no," they also need to learn to accept "no" as a valid answer and not feel rejected or hurt. Practice using the phrase "no means no" in your classroom.

Willpower

Ask a variety of questions for which the students will answer "No" in unison for practice. After several questions, have the students read the Willpower statement aloud together.

Lesson 15

Materials
My Best Me textbook, writing utensils, paper, journal, audiovisual equipment

Resources
Student Worksheet: 4yu.info/?i=98415
Parent Summary: 4yu.info/?i=98465
Video: S.M.A.R.T goals - Link: 4yu.info/?i=94141

Glossary
motivate, accomplished, tasks, focus, reward, jump-start, proactive, vision, stress-free, anxious, prioritize, compare, reasonings

Motivation
Motivation is the mechanism that drives us to accomplish tasks each day. It is like a muscle that can be built up and exercised by consistently doing some basic steps: structuring and organizing life, writing things down, motivational self-talk and celebrating small and big wins. Internal motivation is the key to success in the real world.

Each day, students are faced with a variety of tasks, in and out of school, that need to be accomplished. They will need an inner drive to accomplish each task in due time and with excellence. Students need to know the power and value of self-motivation. It will give them a feeling of satisfaction, dignity, accomplishment and help them develop a healthy, can-do attitude. They will experience internal victories as well as external rewards as they become committed to others as well as to themselves.

As the students become more responsible, it is essential that they learn to organize tasks and figure out on their own how to get everything done without feeling overwhelmed. Sometimes they may not enjoy doing certain things, but it is important that they learn to complete their work and take responsibility. One way to ensure this process is to teach them to be organized on a daily basis. The following suggested link is a simple and clear explanation of S.M.A.R.T goals that they can use to help plan and accomplish their tasks in a timely fashion. 4yu.info/?i=94141

15 What Motivates Me?

Goal To learn how to <u>motivate</u> myself to do and finish tasks I don't like

Pathways

Observe

Behind each action that we do well is a motivation. Motivation is the desire or willpower inside of us to do something. It can be compared to an inner force that drives us to get tasks <u>accomplished</u>. Look at the following situations and write the motivation that might be needed to accomplish each activity.

_____   _____   _____
_____   _____   _____

Comment

Look again at the images. Are the people in each picture enjoying what they are doing? Think about your daily activities. Do you like everything you have to do each day? Name a few <u>tasks</u> you dislike doing: _____
Why do you dislike these tasks? How do you accomplish tasks that you dislike doing?

Understand

At times, we have more motivation to get things done than at other times. Often, when we do not enjoy doing something, we try to avoid it, postpone it or maybe even ask someone to do it for us. However, avoiding something we do not want to do does

40

Goal

Students will learn how internal motivation can help them do things even when they dislike doing them. They will discover what motivates them

Pathways

Observe: Students will write down what they think is motivating each person in the pictures. Explain the definition of motivation. It is an inner force born out of need, desire and willpower that drives us to do things. Some reasons for being motivated are to fulfill a need, feel satisfied or worthy, serve others, find success, make money, etc. Motivation is mostly needed when we do not feel like doing certain tasks.

Comment: Use these questions to help guide a general class discussion. Have the students imagine

not solve the problem. In the end, we still have to do it.
Putting it off just creates more stress and anxiety.

A clear vision of what needs to get done will motivate us to focus on the necessary tasks as soon as we can, and accomplish all our tasks each day. Think about working smarter, not harder. Perhaps your motivation is a reward, for example, telling yourself that if you finish cleaning your room by the weekend, you can invite your friends over for a visit. Though motivation can come from inside, there's nothing wrong with adding a reward to the process to jump-start your motivation. Motivation is like a muscle; we can build it up through some simple steps:

1. Set short-term and long-term goals
2. Tell yourself that you can and will complete the tasks
3. Celebrate accomplishments because it feels good to reach your objectives
4. Be self-motivated and proactive to accomplish your vision and stay stress-free.

 Activity

Leah feels anxious because she just arrived home from school and has a lot to do. Help Leah prioritize her tasks with 1 being the most important, and 8 being the least important.

____ Take the dog on a walk   ____ Study for a test 3 days from now   ____ Watch TV
____ Call her grandmother   ____ Clean bedroom and bathroom   ____ Eat dinner
____ Go to basketball practice   ____ Do homework for the next day

Comment

Compare your list with 2 or 3 classmates and observe if there are any differences. Share your thoughts and reasonings with each other.

Reflect

How should I prioritize the activities I need to do after school today?

Willpower

I will build up my motivation because it is important for organizing my life and accomplishing my tasks.

41

---

they are doing those tasks. How would they feel about completing each task or similar tasks? Discuss what might have motivated each person to accomplish their task, despite any negative feelings about it. For example, the motivation to doing chores is to have a clean place to live, to make your parents happy or proud, or to receive a reward. Motivation to do our homework might be to get good grades, to develop our intelligence, or to please our teachers or parents. Finally, motivation to exercise is to stay healthy and have more energy during the day and to sleep better at night. In all of these situations, motivation is helping that person finish the task at hand.

Briefly discuss tasks that students have to accomplish each day. Talk about which tasks they enjoy doing and which tasks are not as enjoyable and why.

Understand: Have a student summarize what was read. Have another student explain the meaning of motivation. Talk about how having intrinsic motivation from the inside helps us accomplish things that are difficult. We are motivated to finish tasks promptly

because it makes us feel good on the inside, not because an adult is telling us to do it. It will make us feel accomplished, satisfied, and worthy when we complete a task. A lot of tasks at hand can be stressful to finish, especially things that we do not enjoy doing. A smart strategy is to prioritize our tasks so we can finish the most important things first. When we are not motivated to do things and they are left undone, it can overwhelm and stress us more than what is healthy.

Activity: The students will help Leah figure out what she should accomplish first (as the most important), and what can wait until the others are done (the least important.) This is to help students discover their own list of daily tasks that they need to put in order to accomplish.

Comment: Have student's share Leah's list, to compare it with one another. If the students disagree, have them justify their reasons with their group members. It is okay for students to have different reasons on how they organized their lists, as long as they can justify and put into words their thinking processes. Once they have shared with each other, use the rest of the comment questions to reflect on their own lives. What would their own to-do list look like? How did they help Leah organize her life? How can they better organize their own life?

Reflect: Students will create their own to-do list according to the activities they are required to accomplish each day. Start with their busiest day. They will then prioritize their to-do list just like they did with Leah's. The goal is for the students to become more productive.

Willpower

Ask each student to think of a 1-word answer to the question, "What motivates you to do your best?" Ask that question of each student, let them share their answer and,then, have everyone read the Willpower statement aloud together.

Lesson 16

Materials

My Best Me textbook, writing utensils, paper, journal, computer or books for research

Resources

Student Worksheet: 4yu.info/?i=98416
Parent Summary: 4yu.info/?i=98466

Glossary

Venn diagram, comparing, contrasting, similarities, variations, dynamic, harmony, impressive, unite, common, culture, characteristics, traditions, religion, stunning, originate

Motivation

Students have probably already had experience with people from different cultures, religions and backgrounds that make up their communities. These influences impact the perspectives and ideas people have. It is unimaginable to think what planet Earth would be like if every person were exactly the same and there was absolutely no variety.

It is interesting to observe that very young children accept varieties and differences as something common; no questions asked. However, when we grow older, differences can be experienced as uncomfortable and threatening. It is important that students are aware of their thinking processes toward their own background, as well as of the backgrounds of others. When we are open to learning about others, we can learn a lot and create harmony or a work of art in our surroundings. Many students do not know much about their peers' families and cultures, and maybe some even have little insight into their own background and culture. Generally, students tend to notice more superficial differences such as hair, skin color, clothing, etc.

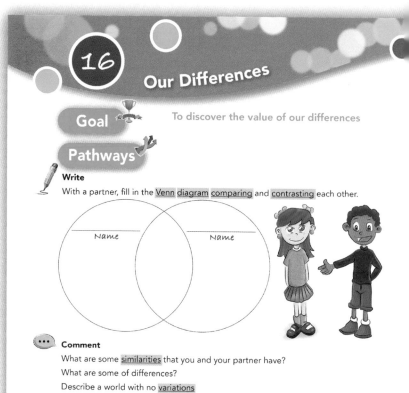

16 Our Differences

Goal To discover the value of our differences

Pathways

Write
With a partner, fill in the Venn diagram comparing and contrasting each other.

Name   Name

 Comment
What are some similarities that you and your partner have?
What are some of differences?
Describe a world with no variations

Understand
When we listen to a song , we can hear different musical instruments working together making different sounds; each instrument giving something special and valuable to the song. If we remove just one instrument, the whole dynamic changes since the instruments have to work together in harmony to create the music. The same happens with a painting. Each stroke and color adds to the impressive end result. Something similar happens when people unite in spite of their differences to do something for the

44

Goal

Students will learn more about each other's backgrounds to enhance their ability to work and live together in harmony, embracing differences instead of judging them

Pathways

Write: Put students into pairs and instruct them to fill in the Venn diagram. If the students have never used a Venn diagram before, give a quick overview of how they work. Each student will label a circle with one of their names. They will write their differences on the outer sides of the circles. They will write what they have in common on the insides of the circles where there is a cross section. The students will naturally notice physical similarities and differences such as hair and eye color, height, and gender. Later in the lesson, they will have the

common good. Each community operates in a similar way. Each person, with their unique culture (the characteristics of a group of people that include language, traditions, religion, food, habits, art), is a valuable part of the whole. When all of these different individuals work together to form a community, something stunning is created, just like a song or painting. Life is more interesting with all our differences. We have a lot to learn and experience from each other and that is an exciting journey.

 Activity: Research
Every family has a different background and culture. Talk to your family about your culture. Where did your family originate? Research your family's background to find information that you can share with your class.

 Comment
What new information did you learn about your family's background?
What are some traditions unique to your culture/family?

 Apply
Go back to the Venn Diagram that you filled in. Look at it again. How are you and your partner similar and different? Do you have the same traditions, religion, language or other cultural experiences? Discuss the similarities and differences between you and your classmates. You can add these characteristics to the Venn Diagram.

 Reflect
What were you able to learn about your classmates from this lesson?
What were you able to learn about yourself from this lesson?

 Willpower
The amazing variety of people in the world creates in me the desire to understand and appreciate myself and others better.

My family

45

---

opportunity to look a little deeper.

 Comment: Encourage each group to share at least one similarity and one difference they observed. Have the students take a minute to imagine if we were all exactly the same. What are some problems that we might run into?

Understand: You could begin by listening to a piece of music from an orchestra and identifying the different sounds that are heard. Each instrument makes a unique sound and, when all of these sounds are combined, it creates beautiful music. If you remove an instrument, the sound changes. This is the same as our community. Every person comes in with a different background and culture, bringing their "sounds and colors." We are all integrally connected and we can come together to make something powerful and significant. When we take the time to learn more about each other, going beyond physical appearances, we can learn a lot. Knowing more about each other will help us accept and understand the people around us as well as ourselves.

Activity: Students may not know much about their own family's background. This research will help the students discover more about their culture so they can better understand themselves and others. The students will interview their families and research their own background and culture. They should understand that culture is the accumulation of characteristics of a particular group of people that includes language, traditions, religion, food, habits, art, etc. Here are some questions to help them prepare: Which languages does your family speak? What holidays does your family celebrate? What kind of foods do you eat as a family? What, if any, religious beliefs does your family follow? All of these aspects are a special part of who you are. The students will write down any information that they discover about their family and culture in their journal or workbook.

Apply: With the same partner, the student will add to the Venn diagram the similarities and differences that go beyond appearance. This is a great opportunity for students to learn new things about each other. Encourage the students to have a meaningful and respectful conversation with each other by asking questions. Invite students to bring one object or something significant that can help express unique aspects about their culture.

Reflect: Ask students what they experienced as they learned more about themselves and others. Learning about each other, enhances understanding of each others' perspectives and ideas. This should increase the acceptance of things that might otherwise be strange and unusual to us.

Willpower

Students will have a greater appreciation for variety and differences. They will grasp the fact that respecting others' traditions and beliefs is the key to living in harmony.

Lesson 17

Materials
My Best Me textbook, writing utensils, paper, journal, bottle of glue or other weight, tape, index cards, ruler

Resources
Student Worksheet: 4yu.info/?i=98417
Parent Summary: 4yu.info/?i=98467

Glossary
measuring tape, collaboratively, efficient, designing, concentrate, contributes

Motivation
Working collaboratively is a skill that students will need to use throughout their lives. They need to learn how to be able to successfully work with others in school, at home and in the workplace. Students will discover how each individual has a unique skill set of skills and different perspective. The joining of the different skills sets and perspectives strengthens any project or task. The benefit of working collaboratively is to capitalize on the strengths of each individual in the group. One might be strong in an area in which another is weak. We can be more successful and efficient when we work together with others.

Knowing our strengths and weaknesses will create confidence and clarity and help us when we contribute in group activities and tasks. We will be more successful when are strategic in working with others. Sometimes it can be difficult to work together. At times, it may seem easier to make all the choices and complete the work alone. Sometimes people are unpleasant and hard to work with and we do not enjoy their company. Whether we like it or not, collaboration is an important part of everyday life. As difficult as others might be in working together, we should strive to enhance who we are in team work and activities. It will open doors for us that we would have not been able to walk through otherwise.

17 I Am a Team Player

 Goal To understand how to work together effectively to achieve a common goal

 Pathways

Activity
Imagine building a birdhouse. What do you need to build it? Make a list of the tools and the materials you will use and explain how you will use each tool.

Tool	How will you use that tool?

Comment
How does each tool play a role in building the birdhouse?
What challenges might you face without having all of the tools available?
Would you be successful using just one tool?

Understand
When we build something, all of the different tools have a unique role in helping us achieve our goal. The hammer is used for pounding the nails. The saw is used for cutting the wood. The nails and glue are used to hold the materials together. The measuring tape is used to make everything the correct size. Without all the tools, we would not be able to successfully complete the job.

46

Goal

Being a team player is the ability to recognize and value the unique skills and abilities each individual brings to the table to complete a task or challenge together

Pathways

 Activity: What list of materials and tools are needed to build a birdhouse? Students will give an explanation of the purpose of each item on their list. Students should gain insight as they understand that to complete this project, they need each of the tools for different yet very significant reasons. Without all the tools and materials, the project would be difficult or even impossible to complete.

As the students share their answers, make a chart similar to the one provided. Use the chart so students

This is similar to working <u>collaboratively</u> with a group of people. Everyone in the group has a different set of skills that can help complete a task. Our many different abilities and perspectives make working together very <u>efficient</u> and successful, if we are willing to cooperate with each other. Some people excel in math while others are handy with tools or <u>designing</u>. When we work collaboratively, we use our strengths to benefit the group. When we <u>concentrate</u> on all of our strengths, we create the best work.

Write

When we work in a group, we use our areas of strength to help the group. Write three areas of strength that you have.

1. _____
2. _____
3. _____

Apply

- Divide into small groups of 3 or 4
- Use index cards and tape to build a tower that is at least 2 feet tall and can hold a bottle of glue.

Reflect

How did you collaborate with your team?
Did you recognize any areas of weakness in yourself that a teammate helped you with?
What skills did you use to help your team be successful?
Did you have the impression you and your classmates were working together as a team?
Give some clear examples of where you experienced teamwork in this activity.
Give one example of a difficulty you encountered working together as a team.

Willpower

I know how valuable teamwork is, especially when everyone <u>contributes</u> their strengths.

47

Tool/Material	How will you use this for the birdhouse?
Hammer	To secure the nails
Saw	To cut the wood
Nails	To join the wood together
Glue	To hold the wood together
Tape measure	To measure length/width of the boards
Screws	To make the birdhouse solid
Drill	To install the screws
Wood	To create the structure of the birdhouse

can visualize how each tool/material is necessary for the birdhouse, and plays an important role in the process.

Comment: Now use the birdhouse analogy and compare it to teamwork. Let students think of examples of great teamwork and the results of working together.

Understand: The same concept learned from the birdhouse is true for groups of people working in unison. Just like each of the tools has a purpose, so every person has a unique set of skills and abilities that are valuable to the process of completing a task or accomplishing a job. Working in a group is so beneficial because it brings our skills together to get a task done more efficiently and successfully. Working together simply means we capitalize on everyone's strengths.

Write: Encourage your students to think about their own strengths and weaknesses. What can they contribute? How can others contribute to help in their areas of weaknesses? The students will write three of their personal strengths valuable to teamwork. This can be a skill or a personality trait. Guide students to recognize traits that are their strengths. By giving examples, students can think of some of their own. If your students are struggling to identify their strengths, brainstorm as a class and write ideas on the board, or have them work with a partner to discover their strengths.

Apply: The students will engage in a STEM activity working together. If you do not have the materials for the one in the workbook, feel free to use any STEM activity that encourages students to work together. Divide them into small groups of 3-4 students. Remind the students of your classroom rules and procedures for working together. The students will use the materials provided to build a two-foot-tall tower that can hold the weight of a glue bottle. It is up to them to decide how they will design and create their structure. Encourage the students to use their strengths to complete the task. Just like the tools, each member is needed to complete the activity.

Reflect: Evaluate how their team worked together as a group and if they were able to accomplish the given task. Did they enjoy working together?

Willpower

Have the students read the Willpower statement aloud together and end with saying their individual teamwork strength out loud.

Lesson 18

Materials
My Best Me textbook, writing utensils, paper, construction paper, journal, access to Internet, crayons and markers

Resources
Student Worksheet: 4yu.info/?i=98418
Parent Summary: 4yu.info/?i=98468

Glossary
label, roles, waste management, mechanics, productively, explore, brochures

Motivation
A community is a group of people who live, work, and play together and share common interests and goals. All the members of the community contribute and cooperate to achieve certain goals and fulfill common desires.

Though our students may not realize it, they are part of many different communities. Their communities are their classroom, school, sport teams, clubs, places of worship, and neighborhoods. Being part of a community, implies that each individual plays an important role in the community's success. They do this by following the rules and expectations set up for that community, and by contributing their skills and abilities, by being open and sensitive to the needs of others. Your students will learn how to contribute to their communities by helping others when needed.

Your students are now at a level of growth and age where they can begin to be sensitive of the needs of others and find ways to help. It is valuable for them to learn how to become active members and do their part, as well as appreciate and understand the value of other people in their communities and the roles they play.

Goal

To learn what communities are about and to be willing to participate and be responsible, for their common wealth and health

Pathways

Read/Write: Students need to understand what a community is. They will draw a picture of two communities they belong to; their school community and their neighborhood community. Refer back to the definition of community.

Comment: Discuss the communities the students chose and the unique characteristics of each one. For example, in a school community, the goal of the members is education; in a neighborhood community, the goal of the members is pleasant, comfortable living conditions.

a community function smoothly. We have doctors to keep us healthy, <u>waste</u> <u>management</u> workers to pick up our trash, car <u>mechanics</u> to fix our vehicles and caregivers to watch children while their parents work. We live <u>productively</u> because of these people. In order for a community to be successful, each one of us is responsible to do our part. Children can contribute, too. For example, we should all take care of our classroom, listen to each other, follow the rules, and be kind to one another. Children can also serve an elderly neighbor by shoveling snow or mowing the lawn. At home, they can cooperate by raking leaves or putting the dishes away. Everyone, both big and small, should do their part in their community.

Activity

The class will do a service project together to better the community. This project will be something that helps the community in an area of need. Take some time to <u>explore</u> different projects and vote on your class favorite! Our class service project will be

_____

My service project ideas

Create

Create posters, <u>brochures</u>, etc. to hang up around the school and encourage people to help support your project!

Reflect

How did your project make a difference in your community?
What responsibility or service did you take on in the project?
How does your community help you?

 Willpower

I serve my communities with my skills and abilities to create a better place to live.

49

Have students brainstorm what role they play in their communities by focusing on what "gift" they share together. This might be a little tricky, because some may not realize what they can contribute to their communities. Help students think outside the box and find ways that they can impact their community. For example, thank the garbage man for removing the garbage, or the janitor for keeping the school clean, etc. Any answers they come up with are great. Write things down on the board; perhaps make a list of their communities, their points of interest, and the roles students play in those communities.

Understand: Discuss the communities to which students belong, and their responsibilities inside those communities. Have students share about what makes the classroom a community. Does everyone have to work together to ensure learning is taking place? Is everyone kind and respectful toward one another? Who is responsible for keeping the classroom clean and orderly? Encourage them to think about how they can help others in the classroom. If someone needs a piece a paper or if someone forgets their lunch, what do they do? In a

community, all of its members take care of each other.

Activity: The students will research and brainstorm ideas for a service project that the class will complete together. The goal of the service project is to benefit one of the communities in which they are involved. Are students familiar with any service projects that have taken place in their communities? Give some examples. Make sure that this service project is something that will tangibly benefit the school or the nearby neighborhood. They could talk to the principal and discover something that the school can use. Guide the students to brainstorm ideas and use their creativity to attend to others in their community. Some ideas include collecting winter gear for the homeless; collecting food or toys for underprivileged children; collecting supplies for an animal shelter, etc. The class will vote on one project to complete together; then they will organize and plan their community service project.

Create: Students' posters can be put on display around the school to promote the project. Establish due dates for when the collection items need to be turned in. Let them get a taste of what it is like to complete a service project from start to finish.

Reflect: Discuss together the impact the project had on the community. The students can also think about how others in the community helped them.

 **Willpower**

Help the students to recognize two things we all have to contribute: time and attention. Ask the students to pledge their time and attention to find their place of contribution in their communities.

Lesson 19

Materials
My Best Me textbook, writing utensils, paper, blindfold, markers, crayons

Resources
Student Worksheet: 4yu.info/?i=98419
Parent Summary: 4yu.info/?i=98469

Glossary
trust, interact, betrayed, vulnerable, trustworthy, token

Motivation

The people you know is one of the most important aspects of life, because they help to shape and form us. They create opportunities for us and add great significance to our life.

Students will understand that in life, they will meet many different kinds of people in a great variety of circumstances. Some of these people will become close friends, while most of the others will be acquaintances, work colleagues, or casual friends. The people we are the closest to are the ones we trust the most. When we trust someone, we feel safe and comfortable around that individual and share with them more of ourselves.

We know that these people will always be there for us, and will protect and support us during difficult times. Trust is something that takes a while to build and, (unfortunately) can be lost in a moment. When we first meet someone, we tend to be cautious and distrustful. It is important that students recognize and discern the people around them whom they can trust, what they can entrust them with and the people to stay away from.

19   My Circle of Trust

Goal   To recognize who is in my circle of <u>trust</u> and why they are there

Pathways

 Game

Where am I going?
- Find a partner and take turns.
- One student will put a blindfold over their eyes.
- The student will be gently spun around three times.
- Then the student that can see will lead the blindfolded partner around, keeping them safe.

 Comment

How did you feel when you were blindfolded?
Did you trust the person who was leading you around? Why or Why not?
How did it feel to be the eyes for someone who could not see?

Understand

People all around us can be our friends; those we have known for years or those we just met. With each of these individuals we <u>interact</u> differently based on the level of trust we have in them. It can take a while to trust someone, but when we do, we know they will support us and keep us safe no matter what. On the other hand, once someone has <u>betrayed</u> us, trust generally will be instantly lost.

In today's activity, you had to trust your partner to keep you safe when you were <u>vulnerable</u> because you could not see. If your partner let you bump into something, you probably lost trust in them. The people that we rely on make up our circle of trust. These are the people who care about us, people who don't judge us, and the people we can go to for support and comfort at all times.

50

Goal

Healthy relationships are built upon serving one another, mutual respect, and trust. The students will participate in a trust-building activity and reflect on their circle of trust

Pathways

Game: Students will experience in person what trust is. Emphasize that they treat each other with great care. One student will blindfold their partner, turn them around three times, and safely lead them around the classroom or playground. Switch roles so each student has the opportunity to lead. You can increase the challenge by having students do it in silence.

Comment: Discuss how the activity went and have students describe how they felt when they were blindfolded, as well as how they felt being the leader.

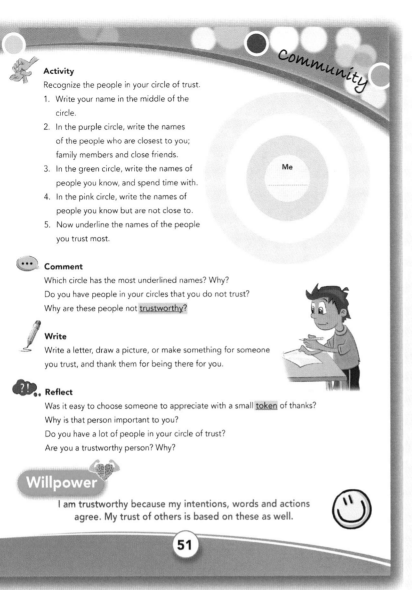

Activity

Recognize the people in your circle of trust.

1. Write your name in the middle of the circle.
2. In the purple circle, write the names of the people who are closest to you; family members and close friends.
3. In the green circle, write the names of people you know, and spend time with.
4. In the pink circle, write the names of people you know but are not close to.
5. Now underline the names of the people you trust most.

Comment

Which circle has the most underlined names? Why?

Do you have people in your circles that you do not trust?

Why are these people not trustworthy?

Write

Write a letter, draw a picture, or make something for someone you trust, and thank them for being there for you.

Reflect

Was it easy to choose someone to appreciate with a small token of thanks?

Why is that person important to you?

Do you have a lot of people in your circle of trust?

Are you a trustworthy person? Why?

Willpower

I am trustworthy because my intentions, words and actions agree. My trust of others is based on these as well.

51

How trustworthy are they as a friend? Students should experience what trust is from both sides. If they want others to trust them, they need to behave like someone they would trust. Students should understand that their own trustworthiness includes their thoughts, actions and words. When they need advice, direction or counsel, whom do they go to for guidance and why?

Understand: Have the class define trust and write it on the board or chart paper as a reference. Trust is being reliable, dependable, authentic, sincere, upright, honorable and honest. Trust is built over time and through experiences; we do not usually automatically trust the people around us. It is a process in which we observe that the actions and words of an individual are in consistent agreement.

The flip side is that trust can be broken very easily in comparison to the effort it takes to build. Have the students think about the people they trust the most, and how those people have earned their trust. Feel free to have students share personal experiences about

trust built or lost. Keep the discussion constructive and positive. You can get the discussion started by sharing a story from your own life that is appropriate and relevant for this age group.

Activity: The students will visualize their circle of trust by writing down the names of the people they know in the appropriate circles. When the students have underlined the names of the people they trust, have them observe in which circle most of these people are located. Are these the people they can go to if they need support, guidance or help?

Comment: Have your students reflect on the people in their circle of trust. Discuss as a class if there are any people in their inner circle who did not get underlined. Sometimes there are people close to us who we do not trust. Be alert and take note if certain individuals are not in the student's trust circle who commonly should be there. If that student is struggling at school or with their peers, discuss this exercise with a social worker or counselor to investigate further with the student.

Write: The students will write a nice letter, draw a picture, or make a gift for someone in their circle of trust. They will learn the value of showing their appreciation, through small acts of kindness, for the people in their circle of trust.

Reflect: Look back at the definition of trust the class made together and have each student evaluate their trustworthiness.

Willpower

Students should be motivated to be trustworthy. They should also be able to clearly identify the people in their life whom they can trust.

Lesson 20

Materials
My Best Me textbook, writing utensils, paper, markers, crayons

Resources
Student Worksheet: 4yu.info/?i=98420
Parent Summary: 4yu.info/?i=98470

Glossary
Internet, research, privacy, resources, astute, public server, cyberworld, monitor, logging, limits

Motivation

In today's society, the Internet plays a large role in our daily lives. We use it to search for information, connect with others, play games, and do work. This is not any different for children. They have had the Internet around their entire lives. They use it on a daily basis for the same reasons adults do.

Moreover, it can be a great resource when used appropriately. Most children are overly comfortable and confident using the Internet, and tend to think they know how to adequately handle the great variation of programs and apps. However, many youth don't understand how many sites and links are used to entice them and lure them into making some kind of commitment, releasing private information, collecting data (spy ware) or exposing them to dangers. It is very important that your students learn to set up viable boundaries of Internet usage to improve Internet safety. It is our job as adults to teach them these parameters, and closely supervise them in that process. This lesson will be a starting point to help students learn the importance of safe Internet use, and how to protect their privacy while on-line.

An idea might be to allow them to research Silicone Valley moguls and how they allow their children to use devices as well as the Internet.

Goal   To learn to use the <u>Internet</u> in a wise, safe and efficient manner

Pathways

Activity - Survey

Read each question. Circle your answer. (Thumbs up for yes; thumbs down for no)

👍 👎	I use the Internet on a daily basis
👍 👎	I use the Internet to send and receive emails
👍 👎	I use the Internet to <u>research</u>
👍 👎	I use the Internet to play games
👍 👎	I use the Internet to listen to music
👍 👎	I use the Internet to watch videos
👍 👎	I use the Internet to chat with my friends
👍 👎	I use the Internet to tell my stories and share my pictures

💬 **Comment**

Does the Internet play a role in your daily life? How?
What is <u>privacy?</u> How do you protect your privacy on the Internet?
Do you abide by safety rules in how you use the Internet? Which ones?

💡 **Understand**

The Internet has become a large part of our daily lives. We use it to communicate, learn, listen to music, and play games. The Internet is a great <u>resource</u> to have, however, there are hidden dangers to using the Internet that we should be aware of to become <u>astute</u> and stay safe.

- How do we deal with our personal and private information?
- What do we do when we use a <u>public server</u>?
- What do we put on the Internet?
- Who are we connecting with?

52

Goal

The students will be able to identify some of the pros and cons of social media as they evaluate and reflect upon the frequency and manner of their own Internet use

Pathways

Activity: The students will fill in the survey giving each thought the thumbs up or thumbs down. You could enhance the activity by giving students the opportunity to make a list of all social networks or gaming platforms they use. Then have them identify how much time they spend on them, including what type of messages, information and images they post and games they play. Encourage students to think carefully about the type of personal information they are sharing on-line, and with whom they are sharing it as well as why they share. Most of the time,

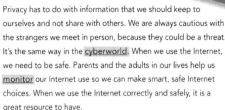

Privacy has to do with information that we should keep to ourselves and not share with others. We are always cautious with the strangers we meet in person, because they could be a threat. It's the same way in the cyberworld. When we use the Internet, we need to be safe. Parents and the adults in our lives help us monitor our Internet use so we can make smart, safe Internet choices. When we use the Internet correctly and safely, it is a great resource to have.

Apply - Safe or Unsafe

Read each scenario. If it is a safe Internet usage, color it green for "go." If it is an unsafe Internet usage, color it red for "stop."

Logging off after using your computer	Sharing pictures of yourself on the Internet	Playing games on the Internet with your friends
Showing an adult something that made you feel uncomfortable on the Internet	Opening an email from someone you do not know	Telling someone your first and last name
Sending an email to your friend	Doing research on your favorite animal using Google	Talking to somebody you do not know

Comment

What limits have been set for your Internet usage?

What can you do if you are uncomfortable with something happening on the Internet, or with something you might have done?

Reflect

Make a list of Internet rules with your family. Hang these rules in your house where everyone can see them.

What are your thoughts and feelings concerning the rules you have written down? Why?

Willpower

I protect myself by using the Internet wisely and safely.

53

---

media. It might also open up a possibility for students to discuss and comment on the points mentioned and influence each other to better use the devices and the access they have.

 Comment: Let this discussion motivate students to do something different, to stand out. If approved by the parents, and resources are available, let the students start a movement by posting positive ideas on the social networking sites, with the students holding each other accountable. If students are not permitted to use social media (or do not have access), consider doing a special class post that could be temporarily added to the school's website or social networking page such as inspirational quotes or tips for appropriate social media use, etc.

Reflect: Today's lesson is a hot topic among early adolescents and presents a perfect opportunity to discuss real life social issues in the students' lives. It should motivate students to analyze their own use of social media and encourage children to form their own educated opinions on the topic. The more credit we give our students by recognizing their ability to make wise and informed decisions, the greater the chance that they will live according to those expectations.

---

the why is more powerful than the what and how.

Comment: The questions serve as a guide for the students to self-reflect and determine the amount of time they spend on social media, and their purpose for using it. It is a back-up to support the activity they just completed.

Understand: Read this section with the students and allow them to discuss in small groups, or as a class, their thoughts and opinions on social media and Internet use. The students may also have personal insights to share that may encourage their peers to share their experiences.

Apply: The students will mark the chart with what is a safe and secure way of dealing with the Internet and what are unsafe and dangerous ways. Review their answers and have them explain to the class why they marked it the way they did. If time allows, draw two columns on the whiteboard with benefits and dangers of social media, networking and the Internet. This will create a clear picture of the double sided effects of social

Willpower

Students have a better understanding of why there are rules for using the Internet safely, and how these boundaries help protect their privacy.

Lesson 21

Materials
My Best Me textbook, writing utensils, paper, markers, crayons, paper cut into heart shapes, A backpack and a heavy object for each student to drop into the pack

Resources
Student Worksheet: 4yu.info/?i=98421
Parent Summary: 4yu.info/?i=98471

Glossary
resolve, conflict, discussed, burdens, release, excuse

Motivation

Life can be hard, and pain is unavoidable. However, there are tools we can provide to our students to help them deal with conflict in a healthy manner. How we deal with conflict determines how peaceful we live our lives. If we can forgive and forget hurts and offenses, we will get rid of burdens and live in greater harmony. The earlier in life we learn the benefits of asking and giving forgiveness, the more peace we will experience. Sometimes it takes time and practice to forgive people.

It can help students have a meaningful connection to think about their past experiences. Of course, the question arises: "How do I forgive someone who hurt me?" It is a simple decision to say it aloud and express forgiveness, releasing that individual from their debt from wrong-doing. Acting on this decision will probably not remove the pain or emotion connected to the wrong-doing, but those spoken words start to affect our thinking process and, eventually, how we feel. When thoughts arise to remind us of the hurt, we must remember and reinforce our decision to forgive. This decision to forgive will allow others to forgive us when we hurt others. We all make mistakes and we all need forgiveness. To forgive and to ask for forgiveness requires humility, which is to be unpretentious, mild and modest.

Goal To learn the best ways to resolve conflict and live in peace

Pathways

Write

All through life we will have both positive and negative experiences with others. Write about a negative interaction that you have had with another person. What happened? How did you feel during the interaction? Has the difference been resolved? How? How did you feel after it was discussed?

_____
_____
_____
_____

Game - Heavy Burdens?

Walk around the room once with an empty backpack or a grocery bag, (if you do not have a backpack). Everyone puts a heavy book or similar heavy object in their neighbor's backpack and walk around the room again. Repeat this process until everyone's backpack is full. Imagine each of the books is a negative interaction that you have had with someone. The more books (or conflicts), the heavier the backpack is to carry.

Comment

How did the backpack feel at the beginning versus at the end?
Do you go through life with a "heavy backpack" due to unpleasant or angry interactions with others, or are you able to get rid of the weight by doing all you can to resolve conflicts and release them?

Goal

The students will develop ways to resolve conflict with others so they do not carry the weight of negativity with them

Pathways

Write: Have the students describe a negative interaction they had with another person and how it affected them; how it kept them occupied thinking about it, how they talked about it with other people, how they handled the situation, and how the conflict was resolved (or not). Some examples of conflict could be a verbal fight with another student, an argument with a sibling, a disagreement with a teammate, or a remark on social media. Allow students to share these experiences to set them up for the next step in handling conflict using

Understand

Carrying unresolved burdens or conflicts on the inside of you is just like the backpack full of heavy books. These burdens keep us from having peace on the inside. To get rid of these burdens and keep our peace, it is important to forgive hurtful words and actions of other people. Sometimes our own actions or words hurt the people we love and care about the most, and we always want them to forgive us. We get forgiveness when we have a habit of forgiving others, which always removes the heavy burden on the inside.

How do you forgive others when they do mean or hurtful things to you? Though it may be hard, realize that there is a motivation behind every action. Perhaps that person has an unhappy life at home, or they feel small and unimportant. Does this excuse their mean behavior? No. But it will help you to be mindful of *why* they might be mean and hurtful. If we hold onto our anger, it will only hurt us. But if we can forgive the person, we will walk in greater peace. The way to forgive is to say the words out loud, "I forgive...." The same happens if we carry the burden of regret for hurting someone with our actions or words. We can lift this weight by using our words, asking for forgiveness.

 ## Activity - "The heart of love"

On the heart your teacher gave you, write positive words or actions that can be taken to resolve a conflict. Don't forget by your words you can release yourself and others!

Reflect

Do I carry negativity like a heavy burden?
How do I handle conflict in my life? Do I stuff it down, or deal with it?
Am I able to forgive and forget? Is forgetting sometimes harder than forgiving?
I will practice using the words "I forgive you?" and "Please forgive me?" often.

Willpower

I will do all I can to resolve conflicts in my life so I can live in peace and harmony.

55

---

resolution tools.

Game:
This activity will help students understand what it means to carry a burden. Remind them that each of the weighted objects represents a negative interaction that they have had with another person. The student will walk around a second time, this time a weighted object will be removed from the backpack and handed to a classmate, signifying that each interaction has been resolved and peace has been made.

Comment:
The student with the backpack will explain to the class the difference they felt between an empty and a full backpack. Remind them that the backpack represents their life and the heavy objects the negative interactions and conflicts they have had. This is a bit abstract, so ask the students what the idiom means when you hear, "To carry the weight of the world on your shoulders" or, "To be burdened down with..." It means that you have a lot of things affecting you in a negative way. Have the students reflect on their own lives using the example of the negative interaction they wrote down at

the beginning of the lesson. Did they resolve the conflict or are they still carrying the weight of that incident? Encourage them to forgive everyone involved, so they can let go of that weight. Remind them of the simple steps of how to forgive. Important note: If you suspect any hurts that might have roots in abuse, consult with your supervisor or counselor.

Understand:
To maintain a peaceful life, we need to choose to resolve conflict, forgive others, and ask for forgiveness. This can be difficult to do, depending on how badly we have been hurt or how badly we have hurt the feelings of others. It takes courage and willpower to forgive and ask forgiveness. However, when we do not resolve conflict, we carry those negative thoughts with us every day, which makes it harder to live in peace. The burden or bad feelings take up space in our thoughts and hearts, impacting our emotions and social interactions.

Activity:
Students will write a word or action on a heart that can help resolve conflicts such as, give a hug, forgive, give a compliment, ask to be friends, etc. Once each heart has been filled in, glue all of the hearts onto a larger board to be displayed in the classroom as a reminder of how to resolve conflict in order to promote peace in the classroom.

Reflect:
Encourage students to resolve any lingering conflicts they may have, even if the other party refuses to settle the conflict; they can be friendly and forgive, no matter what. Remind them that they are not responsible for the other person's words or reactions; only for their own.

Willpower

Students should be motivated to resolve conflicts, and have tools to reach resolution peacefully and in a timely manner, with the goal of removing burdens. Create a classroom environment where this is important.

53

Lesson 22

Materials
My Best Me textbook, writing utensils, paper, markers, crayons
* Suggestion: Two great read aloud books to tie to this topic are *Invisible Boy* by Trudy Ludwig, and *Have You Filled a Bucket Today?* by Carol McCloud.

Resources
Student Worksheet: 4yu.info/?i=98422
Parent Summary: 4yu.info/?i=98472

Glossary
kindness, considerate, respectfully, expressions, complimenting, donating, increases

Motivation
When we demonstrate kindness, we show others that they are important and that we care about them. Students should be able to understand that kindness means we attend to the needs of others, are respectful toward them, and do things to make them happy. Kindness not only impacts those around us, but even brings huge change to ourselves, physically and emotionally. Children at this age are still learning how their words and actions impact the people around them.

Due to electronic devices and the influence of those devices on the brain, research has also proven that children who use electronics are less empathetic and kind than those who do not use them. Therefore, teaching and training in kindness is even more important than before.

Set a high standard of expectancy with your students towards kindness in and out of the classroom. With kindness, we will make the world a better place, even for those who hurt others. For example, most bullies do so to compensate for the pain they feel inside. Kindness will help them to heal, so their need to lash out will be diminished.

22   I Am Kind

Goal   To learn how <u>kindness</u> affects us and those around us

Pathways

Observe
Describe what you think is happening under each picture

_____   _____
_____   _____

Comment
Describe interactions between the children in the two pictures.
Look at the their faces. How do you think each child is feeling?
How do you feel when you are kind to others?
How do you feel when you are unkind to others?
How do your actions affect others and yourself?

Understand
When we show others that we care and are concerned about their well-being, we show kindness. Kindness is being <u>considerate</u> with and of others, treating them <u>respectfully</u> and doing nice things for them. When we are kind, we focus on others and do all we can to make them feel happy. As we do so, changes occur inside us physically and emotionally.

56

Goal

Students will learn the impact that being kind has on themselves and others. Kindness is contagious. They will have the opportunity to practice kindness daily

Pathways

Observe: Let the students put into words what they see. Take into consideration how they talk about the two images. Have the class share their thoughts.

Comment: The students should recognize that the first picture is a happy and positive interaction, and the second picture is a negative and mean interaction. How do the students know what is happening without any background knowledge? When we are mean to others, we are not happy on the inside and that shows on the outside. We can learn a lot about what is happening

When we treat others poorly, we feel unpleasant about ourselves and hurt the people around us. However, no matter how we treat people, it will greatly affect how we feel about ourselves.

Kindness is a simple decision that we can make every day by using friendly words and considerate actions. Small expressions of kindness might include saying hello to someone, giving a helping hand or complimenting someone. We can show larger acts of kindness by helping someone with their homework or chores, raising money for a family in need, collecting food for the hungry or donating our toys or clothes we no longer use to those in need. Whether our acts are big or small, showing kindness makes the world a happier place for everyone.

Activity

Fill in the chart with random acts of kindness that you would like to do. When you do the act of kindness, color in that square.

Reflect

How did being kind to others make me feel?
How did my acts of kindness make the other people feel? How could I tell?
What act of kindness had the greatest impact?

Willpower

Being kind makes those around me happy and increases my joy and well-being.

57

What kindness looks like?	What kindness sounds like?
Smiling	I am sorry
Hugging	invitations
Positive	Compliments
Fun	nice words
Caring	cheerful
Listening	No thank you
Extending a helping hand	Please

in a situation when we look at body language and expressions. Ask what kinds of postures, gestures and expressions show kindness and friendliness.

Understand: After reading, talk with the students about what kindness is and what it looks like. Make a chart divided into two sections on the board or chart paper. On the left, write words your students share that describe what kindness looks like; on the other side, write words that describe what kindness sounds like. (See the chart at the top left corner.)

Talk about what being kind does to us and how it makes us feel. Think about the feeling that happens when you give someone a gift. We feel good, but it also increases our joy to see the other person happy. This is the same feeling we get when we are kind to others. The opposite happens when we are unkind to someone. We not only feel bad on the inside, but we also make the people around us feel bad and sad.

Ask students what they can do when someone is unkind, abusive or bullies them or someone they know. What choice would they make? What would help solve the problem? The students should recognize that kindness has better results than being unkind. Also focus on what is known as the "bystander effect;" when we witness someone being hurtful to someone else, but we do nothing to stop it. This can leave us with regret, even though we may not have been an active part of the negative interaction. Ask students to share their thoughts on what they can do if they see someone else being unkind.

Activity: Students will brainstorm random acts of kindness that they can perform daily for others, at school and at home. Remind them that even small gestures bring happiness. Some examples are: saying hello to someone new, greeting the bus driver, making a card or picture for someone, giving a compliment, helping set the table for dinner, letting your brother/sister pick their favorite game; etc. The goal is to make the acts simple and doable. Students should notice that it does not take much effort to make others happy. Encourage them to try to complete all their acts over the next few days. They can color in the corresponding square once they did the act of kindness. Assure students that you observe their acts of kindness. Compliment them for it, in private as well as in public.

Reflect: Wait a couple of days for students to complete their acts of kindness, then talk about their experiences.

Willpower

Students will discover that kindness makes others happy and increases their own joy and creates an environment for learning and growth.

55

Lesson 23

Materials

My Best Me textbook, writing utensils, paper, construction paper, markers, crayons, access to Internet or library
* Suggestion: A book you could use that connects actions and the environment is *What If Everybody Did That?* by Ellen Javernick.

Resources

Student Worksheet: 4yu.info/?i=98423
Parent Summary: 4yu.info/?i=98473

Glossary

environment, envision, surroundings, extent, impacts, significant, gratefulness, attentively

Motivation

Our environment gives us everything we need to survive and enjoy life. It provides the air we breathe, the water we drink, the land that we live on, and the plants and animals we see. It also gives us moments of entertainment, relaxation and refreshment. All of these elements are integral parts of our daily existence that affect us in big and small ways. Often, we take for granted the gifts our environment provides us. We may not see the consequences immediately, nevertheless, each one of us has a valuable role in taking care of our planet.

With this lesson, the students will become aware of some of the impacts they can have on nature, be it positive or negative, as well as what they can do to sustain and strengthen it. They are never too young to make an impact. Moreover, all of our actions count, and will influence how our environment looks now as well as in the future. Because the students are young, making them aware of their role will establish a mindset and habits of appreciation for the environment, so they can enjoy it when they are older.

Focusing these young minds on their environment could, hopefully, stir their passion to discover creative solutions to the challenges Earth faces.

23 Caring for My Natural Environment

Goal To learn to enjoy and take care of my environment

Pathways

 Create
Close your eyes and envision yourself in the perfect outdoor environment. Draw, paint or make a detailed picture showing this environment.

 Comment
What words would you use to describe your picture?
What do you need to do to take care of that environment?
Add to your drawing what happens if we do not care for that environment.
What emotions do you feel in the taking care scenario and the not taking care scenario?

Understand
Our environment is everything that is part of our surroundings. It is the air we breathe, the water we drink, the land we walk and live on, and the plants and animals around us. Our everyday actions of running water, turning on lights, throwing away trash and driving cars affect the environment around us. We have an impact on our environment every day, but we rarely realize the extent of that impact.

60

Goal

The students will learn from each other the different ways the environment impacts them and the way they impact the environment

Pathways

 Create: Give the students an example of how you enjoy the environment. Encourage your students to be creative, use a variety of colors, and include details to bring the story to life. You can model this by drawing your vision to inspire your students.

Comment: Without showing their pictures, have students use adjectives to describe their environment to a partner. This will help them realize how challenging it is to reveal, describe or express the immense beauty and magnitude of nature and the powerful influence

Because we have such a <u>significant</u> effect on our environment, we also have a responsibility to care for it. We can do this by learning how our words and actions affect everything around us and sharing our awareness with others. We can pick up garbage, turn off lights when we leave a room and express our <u>gratefulness</u> for the beauty around us. These are all ways to care for our environment so we can fully enjoy all that it has to offer.

 Activity - Research
Think about the different ways that we may positively or negatively affect our environment. Choose a topic on this subject that interests you to investigate.
My topic is: _____
Research your topic.
Write some notes that you want to remember.

Notes

 Apply
Create a visual aid to share with others to provide awareness on your topic.

 Reflect
What new information did I learn through my research?
How did I share my information with others?
How will this research change my words and actions on regarding my environment?
What is one thing in the environment I greatly enjoy? Why?
What is one thing in the environment I greatly dislike? Why?
What influence does the environment have on me? Why?

 Willpower

I take responsibility for my environment and choose to <u>attentively</u> care for it.

61

---

it has on us. When the students are done, discuss how they can keep their environment the way they imagined it. Next, discuss some things that are happening in our environment that are causing it to either improve or deteriorate. Some examples can be planting trees, effective recycling efforts, rehabilitation of wildlife, pollution, litter, deforestation, etc. Now have the students go back to their pictures and draw how their perfect environment might look if some of the negative things that they mentioned above happened to or in their environment. Have them compare their original picture to the second one. How did their picture change?

Understand: Brainstorm with students about all the positive and negative things people do that affect their environment. We may not see the consequences of the actions of just one person, but imagine what happens if everyone does it. Because of the impact the environment has on us and we on the environment, we need to be well-informed and educated. Coupled with that knowledge, it's critical for us to use a problem-

solving mindset to tackle the challenges we face. The first step is for students to be more appreciative of the sheer joy and pleasure nature brings. Caring for our environment means it will care for us!

Activity: Students will learn more about different ways to protect and enhance the environment, so they can share their knowledge with others. Make a list together of possible topics to choose from: air pollution, deforestation, water pollution, littering, endangered animals, or landfills. Have students individually choose one subject that they would like to learn more about. (If more than one student chooses the same topic, they can research together.) Students will title their topic and use the Internet or books from the library to do their research. Encourage them to take notes on important information that they might like to share with the class.

Apply: Once students complete their research, they will create a visual of their topic to present to the class, sharing what they learned and teaching their classmates. They can present their information in any way they choose: a poster, brochure, book, video or Power Point on the computer. Their presentation should clearly address a specific impact humans have on the environment, some related facts or statistics, and solutions that we can practically apply to improve that aspect of the environment.

Reflect: It is valuable for students to understand that even though they are young, their decisions and actions make an impact, and that now is the time to learn to appreciate and care for the environment. Have them summarize what they learned.

Willpower

Students have learned the value of taking time to thoroughly enjoy their environment and will do their best to impact it in a positive manner.

Lesson 24

Materials

My Best Me textbook, writing utensils, paper, construction paper, milk cartons or a plastic jugs, ribbons, small twigs, paint, old cards, recycled decorating materials such as buttons, string or sequins, or other items they find to reuse, audiovisual equipment

Resources

Student Worksheet: 4yu.info/?i=98424
Parent Summary: 4yu.info/?i=98474
Video: *Starting a School Makerspace from Scratch* - 4yu.info/?i=94231

Glossary

planet, reducing, reusing, recycling, billion, diminish, damage, sustainable, phrase, wisely

Motivation

Without proper care of our planet, we will endanger ourselves by limiting and maybe losing the resources that it offers (such as pure water to drink and clean air to breathe). Our everyday actions affect the Earth in many ways.

Of course, we cannot underestimate the creativity of mankind in finding solutions; we have met and overcome a multitude of challenges throughout history. That is what will be happening with the challenges we face with the environment as well. However, that is not a green card for living obnoxiously and selfishly concerning the environment. Students need to learn to manage all resources with care and wisdom.

One way that we can manage our planet appropriately is by creatively practicing the three R's: Reduce, Reuse, and Recycle. Students will learn how they can do their part by using the three R's to make a difference through re-processing some of the resources they use. It is important that students become aware of their actions and how they affect our planet. Your students have likely already learned about the three R's, so to take it to the next level, challenge them to think out of the box on how they can reduce, reuse and recycle.

24 I Can Use It Again!

Goal To understand why creatively managing used materials helps care for our planet

Pathways

Write

What do the three **R**'s stand for?
What do you think each of the words mean?

_____ _____

Observe

Look at each picture. Label it as an example of reducing, reusing, or recycling.

Comment

Give three other examples of each R, and how you can reprocess products and items.
Do the three R's help our environment? Why?
How do you put the three R's into effect in your daily life?
Which of the 3R's have you applied in your life and how?
What are my thoughts and feelings on applying the 3R's in my life? Why?

62

Goal

The students will broaden their understanding of re-processing items and materials, and in so doing care for planet Earth. This might spark new ideas or inventions

Pathways

Write: The idea is for them to show and tell what they already know, and activate their prior knowledge so you know the foundation to expand upon. Once the students have written their definitions, create one definition that has been agreed upon by everyone. Some examples: Reusing is finding a new purpose for used items; Reducing is producing, consuming and using less; Recycling is separating used items such as paper, glass, aluminum and plastic to be reprocessed.

Observe: Once the definitions are clear, have

Understand

With all the people living on the Earth, (over 7 billion), we need to find creative ways to deal with the trash we are producing in order to diminish the damage to our environment. It is the responsibility of every person to recognize the effect they have and correctly manage the trash they produce.

One way to do this is to apply the three R's: reuse, reduce, and recycle. We can make a difference when we reuse and reduce trash by finding creative and inventive ways to reprocess products such as paper, glass, aluminum and plastic. When something is recycled, it is made into new materials that can be used again. As you participate, you join in a powerful movement to help keep the Earth safe and sustainable for the next generations. How does that make you feel?

Create

Make a recycled bird feeder:

1. Bring in a clean, empty milk carton or plastic jug.
2. Cut a window in the lower section of the carton or jug.
3. Decorate the carton with used materials: scraps of paper, sequins, buttons, ribbons, cloth, etc.
4. Puncture a tiny hole under the window.
5. Find a twig, secure it with glue in the hole for the bird to sit on.
6. Tie a ribbon or a rope at the top.
7. Pour in birdseed and hang it from a tree or in front of a window.

Reflect

Does making a bird feeder out of reused materials help manage resources and preserve the environment? How?

What does the phrase "environmental pride" mean to you? Why?

What other materials can you reuse instead of throwing them away?

Willpower

I reduce, reuse and recycle to do my part in wisely managing our resources.

63

---

the students look at each picture and decide individually if it is reducing, reusing or recycling and why. Compare their answers. 1. The can as a pencil holder - reusing, it was given a new purpose. 2. Paper into the recycle bin - recycling, it can be turned into new paper. 3. Turning off the lights - reducing, decreasing the amount of energy used. 4. Plastic into a recycling bin - recycling, it can be turned into new usable materials. 5. Yard sale - reusing, others use things we no longer need.

Comment: Students consistently applying the three R's is caring for our environment. How do they apply these R's daily in their own lives? Does the school have recycling bins to recycle paper and plastic? Allow students to talk and share their thoughts and ideas.

Understand: Guide students to think about all the trash that they throw away each day. Make it more visual by having students see how much trash is thrown away each day at school. Visit the trash container. Next, imagine the nearly 8 billion people on this Earth and the trash they produce each day. That adds up! When

---

students think about it in a more tangible manner, they will start to understand the challenges we face in processing trash.

Create: The students will get an opportunity to reuse materials collected at home to make a bird feeder. Encourage students to bring used materials for this project. They can only use materials that have been used before. The instructions for making the bird feeder are given in the textbook. The students can use the materials brought from home as well as any other materials provided to create their bird feeders. Hang them in a tree so the class can see the birds. Make it a weekly class activity to fill the bird feeder and admire the birds that come to it. This project can also extend into a bird counting and identifying activity for a science lesson.

Reflect: Brainstorm as a class other items that can be reused to make something for other subjects such as science, math, history, etc. Encourage students to bring in materials, and allow them to create things with their reusable items during indoor recess or free time. If your school doesn't already have a "makerspace," talk with other teachers and members of the school community about creating a space where the children can bring in items. Once up and running, classes or students can go there to create and explore with these no-longer-needed or recycled items. Check out this website for more ideas on creating a makerspace in your school: 4yu.info/?i=94231

Willpower

Students better understand that as they reduce, reuse and recycle materials, they are doing their part to decrease the Earth's waste and use resources wisely.

Lesson 25

Materials
My Best Me textbook, writing utensils, paper, construction paper, access to library books or Internet
* Suggestion: A great book to use if available is *I Wanna Iguana* by Karen Kaufman Orloff.

Resources
Student Worksheet: 4yu.info/?i=98425
Parent Summary: 4yu.info/?i=98475

Glossary
creatures, survive, hydrated, shelter, preventative, interaction, adopting, broader, properly, purchase, persuasive, considered

Motivation

Children ask for pets because animals and pets bring a lot of joy and love to our lives. However, owning a pet requires quite a bit of responsibility, which the children don't yet recognize. When we bring an animal into our home, it can no longer meet its own needs out of its natural habitat, and it becomes our responsibility to provide for the pet. Research is important when a family is considering a new pet. What are the effort, time and finance requirements? Most young children will promise to care for a hoped-for pet, when in reality, most of them will fall short. Around this age, however, students are becoming more responsible and can play an important role in caring for a pet, though they will always need careful supervision.

Owning a pet is actually a great way to teach kids about caring for something besides themselves. When they understand the needs of their pets and properly care for them, pets can provide a family with a lot of joy, as well as an increased understanding of other responsibilities that life brings with it. How students treat animals will be reflected in how they treat other people around them.

My Fur-ever Friends

Goal To understand the responsibility of caring for pets.

Pathways

 Observe
Look at the pictures below. What are some things each of these creatures need in order to survive?

 Comment
Do these creatures have things in common? Please explain.
How do they get their needs met? Who cares for them?
Are wild animals able to meet their own needs?
Are pets able to meet their own needs?

Understand
All living creatures have basic needs that have to be fulfilled in order for them to survive. We need air to breathe, food to give us nutrients, water to keep us hydrated, and shelter to keep us safe and warm. Without having our needs met, we will not survive. Generally, wild animals are able to provide for themselves. They do not need humans to help them survive. Once we take animals into our homes as pets, their needs are no longer met in the wild, and they rely on us to meet those needs for them.

When we decide to make an animal our pet, it is our responsibility to provide its basic needs: shelter, food and water. We must also provide preventative medical care, appropriate space in our home and interaction. Having a pet brings us much love and

64

Goal

To understand the responsibilities and investment of time and money when owning a "pet-friend"

Pathways

Observe: As they observe the images, have students consider what the three creatures have in common, and what each of them needs to survive.

Comment: Students should be able to identify that they all need air, food, water, exercise, connections and shelter to survive. These are the necessities of life. After sharing in small groups, discuss together as a class how all of these needs are met for each picture. A zebra, a wild animal meets its own survival needs in the wild. A zeal of zebras travel together as a group for enjoyment, but it also comes with a lot of responsibility. The process of "acting locally" by adopting a pet in need will give us a broader awareness of the needs of animals worldwide. What a wonderful way to learn!

Activity

Think about a pet that you would like to have.
Research the needs of that pet so you will know how to properly take care of it.

My new pet would be a _____
My pet eats _____
My pet will be kept _____
My pet will need the following care: _____
Make a list of basic supplies you will need to purchase to care for your pet:
_____

Write

Using what you learned about a future pet, write a persuasive letter to your family about a pet that you would like to have.
If you do not want a pet, explain the reasons for your choice.

Reflect

What should be considered before bringing a pet into my home?
Are pets a good fit for every family? Why or why not?
If you have a pet, are you taking care of the pet or someone else? Why?

Willpower

I understand my responsibilities for pets; the effort, time and money necessary to properly care for them.

65

---

their protection and survival; they locate food, water, shelter and recognize danger on their own. People are also responsible for meeting their own needs once they mature. Children rely on their parents to meet their needs and a pet that is taken into a home relies on its owners to meet its needs. It is unable to get food and water on its own in the home. Explain that this is the key difference between a wild animal and a pet.

Understand: Invite the students to share their experiences with owning pets, positive as well as negative. Another option is to invite a veterinarian to come and share with the students how to best care for the pets they own. If time allows, make a class graph of the different pets that are owned within the classroom.

The students need to understand that bringing an animal into their home is a big responsibility, because they have to make sure the animal's basic needs are being met. There is also much more to consider beyond that. As discussed above, does the family have enough money to adequately provide for the animal? Pets can be very expensive when you consider food, basic supplies,

and medical costs. Clearly, purchasing a pet should be something that is discussed and decided upon as a family.

Activity: The students will first think about a new pet that they would potentially like to have in the house. Maybe it's an animal they have never had before and have always been interested in, or it might entail bringing a second pet into the home. The students will take time to research their pet to find out what is required to properly care for it, especially considering the type of home they live in (apartment or home, other pets, allergies, etc.). As an extension, it might be interesting for them to research how much money each item might cost. The students might not completely understand that a large bag of dog food can cost $30.00, or a trip to the vet to get shots can be $300.00. These are the types of things that they need to know ahead of time, before bringing a pet home. Some animals might seem really fun and exciting to have as pets, but after doing some research, students might find that their particular pet choice is unrealistic, too expensive or they do not make good pets.

Write: Using what they have learned, the students will write a persuasive letter to their family for or against getting a new pet. For example, they might say, "I know that dogs need a lot of exercise, so I can be in charge of playing with the dog in the yard after school."

Reflect: Students should answer these questions individually. If you have a class pet, this might be a great opportunity for students to engage in practicing pet care and testing their ability to be responsible. If not a visit to a pet refuge center might be an option.

Willpower

The students will have a more realistic view and understanding of what is involved with bringing a pet into the home. They will also understand the responsibility it takes to properly care for an animal.

Lesson 26

Materials
My Best Me textbook, writing utensils, paper, paper, markers, crayons access to library books or Internet, audiovisual equipment

Resources
Student Worksheet: 4yu.info/?i=98426
Parent Summary: 4yu.info/?i=98476
Video: *Endangered Species: Worth Saving from Extinction?* 4yu.info/?i=94251

Glossary
chain reaction, deforestation, endangered, habitat, extinct, fortunately, prohibit

Motivation
The number of plants and animals on the endangered species list increases each year. There are multiple reasons why animals become endangered, but the number one factor is human impact (through pollution, deforestation, etc.).

Indeed, human impact can have a chain reaction effect on the environment and all of the wildlife that lives within it. An example is the lionfish originally found in the Indo-Pacific. Someone, somewhere, somehow released the lionfish into the Atlantic Ocean, and it is destroying the original wildlife in that part of the globe. This is because the lionfish has no predators in the Atlantic, thus it has disrupted the ecological balance. The python plague in the Florida Everglades is another result of people releasing ill-suited pets and animals into the wild.

Stories like these can educate us on how our actions need to be well-considered and cautious as we interact with nature. It is in our personal interest to find ways to protect the plants and animals around us. Your students are able to understand the cause-and-effect relationship between human behavior and the environment. With knowledge, they will be better equipped at protecting endangered plants and animals, and begin to engage in creative solutions and applications to help solve the existing challenges we face.

26 Endangered Animals

Goal To learn the chain reaction effect my actions have on nature and wildlife

Pathways

 Observe
Look at both pictures.

 Comment
How does the second picture make you feel? Why?
Why might people cut down trees in forests? How can deforestation be prevented?
What do you think happened to the animals that once lived there?

Video: 4yu.info/?i=94251
Take time to watch this clip.

Understand
Every day, more plants and animals are becoming endangered, partially because of the actions of humans. Animals are in danger when their habitat is destroyed

4yu.info /?i=94251

or they are over-hunted by humans (animals do not over-hunt). If we do not protect our wildlife and their natural habitats, they may become extinct all together. Some endangered animals include certain kinds of hummingbirds, African elephants, certain kinds of bees, and red wolves.

66

Goal

The students will learn how their actions affect the natural elements, plants and animals in the environment around them

Pathways

 Observe: The students will compare and contrast the two pictures of a rainforest; one shows the rainforest full of life, and the other shows stumps and the green leaves burned away.

Comment: The pictures give two very different views of what a rainforest might look like. Encourage the students to think about why people might cut down the trees in a rainforest.

Create understanding in the students for the people in those nations. What is life like for farmers who live

Fortunately, we can do our part in helping protect plants and animals from becoming endangered. There are laws that protect certain animals from being hunted completely or during certain seasons. There are also protected areas of land that prohibit people from harming the habitat where animals live. Learn about what animals are endangered in your area, and then share the information with others. You can also visit areas that are protected, and enjoy their beauty.

Activity
Research an endangered animal that might live near you. Discover why this animal is endangered and learn how you can help. Write any information that you find on the space to the right, or on the next page.

Create
Create a piece of art that you can display at school to raise awareness about your endangered animal. Make sure to include the animal's name, picture and how others can help.

Reflect
How can my actions help save plants and animals from becoming endangered? Are there any other ways that I can help these plants and animals?

Let's save the toucan

Willpower
I will do my part to help protect plants and animals from becoming endangered.

67

and work in the hot, tropical forests of the world. What if you had to work in humid hot weather, chopping down your yard with a machete to avoid snakes and alligators, to make space to plant the crops you depend upon to survive? As residents of developed nations, it is easy to judge others for the way they live, or for the decisions they make. Our goal is to provide a full picture so students understand that deforestation, especially in poor tropical nations, is a complex issue that deserves our best thinking, empathy, and understanding. We want to foster a genuine concern for people living in developing nations who struggle for their daily livelihood, and yet at the same time, fully depend on nature and what it gives them. Sustainability is a proven concept; people living in harmony with the environment, and making a living from the richness of the rainforest.

Students need to understand the effects of deforestation, as trees are cut and harvested to create grazing lands, farm land, or sold on the timber market. In many tropical nations, the soil is low in nutrient content, and becomes infertile after a few growing seasons. The

clearing of forests can effect rainfall levels, cause landslides, and lead to flooding, all of which affect the plants and animals that live there.

Video/Understand: Discuss how our actions affect the environment. When we reduce or eliminate animal habitats, over-hunt a species, or move a species from one ecosystem to another, we can cause animals to become endangered. An endangered species is at risk of becoming extinct, which means gone forever. It might be interesting to look up animals or plants that are endangered in your area and why they are in jeopardy. Next, think about ways that humans can help protect these endangered species. We need to be educated, share what we know with others, learn about the laws that protect animals, and visit protected areas to support and enjoy these endangered species.

Activity: The students will choose one endangered animal to research and study. Have a list of animals available. The students can use the library or on-line resources to research their chosen animal. Before researching, discuss important information that they should look for.

Create: The students will create a project (poster, sculpture, brochure, leaflets, etc.) to inform and raise awareness about the endangered species. It should include the name of the animal, a picture, and suggestions on the protection of the animal.

Reflect: The presentations that students prepared can be displayed around the classroom or school to help raise awareness and interest.

Willpower

The students will know how important their part is in protecting endangered plants and animals. Their interest should be a great start for change.

Lesson 27

Materials
My Best Me textbook, writing utensils, paper, markers, crayons, access to Internet

Resources
Student Worksheet: 4yu.info/?i=98427
Parent Summary: 4yu.info/?i=98477

Glossary
item, electronics, possessions, measure, priceless, memories, precious

Motivation
The time that we are given on this Earth is valuable and priceless and often shorter than we imagine. We tend to associate our intrinsic value and being accepted by others with the material items that we own; our clothes, cars, phones or houses. As children age, they begin to notice and compare these material items with their peers by watching the adults in their life. In the upper elementary grades, students will begin to compare the brands of clothing they wear, or who has the most up-to-date electronics.

Having these material things seems to make people feel valued, accepted and popular. Students should discover that life and its true valuable aspects are the people, experiences, and personal fulfillment comprising each and every day. Once they learn to cherish and appreciate the real treasures of their life they might be less likely be caught up in materialism. They need to learn to make the most of their lives by creating memories, fulfilling dreams, and sharing their time and themselves with the people most important to them. Material things will come and go, but memories last a lifetime.

Another aspect is that there is never an end to buying the latest and newest materialistic possession; as soon as you have obtained the ultimate version, a new one is available, better and more efficient. That creates a frustrating and never satisfying feeling inside.

Goal

To learn to value their life based on experiences, personal realization (especially through serving others with their skills and talents,) and memories with others

Pathways

Write: The students will write an estimated value of each object on the price tag attached to it. The goal is for the students to see that the last picture does not have a monetary value attached to it, yet it is a valuable moment in time that can lead to cherished memories.

Comment: To begin, discuss each picture and talk about the value of each object. You can search on-line to get an estimate of how much each object costs. If you would like to make a math connection, you can have the students compare their guesses with the actual

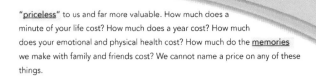

"priceless" to us and far more valuable. How much does a minute of your life cost? How much does a year cost? How much does your emotional and physical health cost? How much do the memories we make with family and friends cost? We cannot name a price on any of these things.

It is important that we make our time on Earth productive. There is great value in spending time and doing activities with the people we love. It is important that we work and have money for the necessities in life such as food, shelter, and clothing. But because life is short and precious, we should direct our attention on spending our precious time where it will yield the most increase; focused on our relationships.

 Create
Do you make the most of your time? Draw a picture and write down your favorite memory.

 Comment
Why was this your favorite memory?
Who was part of your favorite memory?
Did your favorite memory involve people or material items?

Reflect
Can I use my time more wisely? How?
Is there anything I can cut out to make more time for the people and activities that are most important to me?
What do the words "value" and "price" mean to me? How are they different?
Why is time so valuable?

 Willpower

I treasure time, because my time is more valuable than gold.

71

---

value (your own version of "The Price Is Right"). The actual value is not the important aspect of the lesson; but rather, understanding the value of the last picture. Have the students discuss if having a new phone or television would be worth more to them than time with their families or people they love? If there are students with troublesome family situations, you can talk about health; how valuable that is, and what it takes to maintain it.

Understand: Experiences, relationships and personal development are priceless. Many things that we buy give us a certain amount of satisfaction and euphoria. This feeling swiftly vanishes, because we start to want something else, and what we have becomes outdated. Ask them to share about a gift they really wanted and received for their birthday or Christmas last year. Does it still hold the same value for them? Do they even know where it is or still use it?

Help students understand that the material objects that seem so important to them will have little to no importance in a year so. They can begin to evaluate if the

items they have to have urgently at this very moment are really worth it, as opposed to family and friends, fun times, health, peace, etc. To provide ourselves with long-term joy, we need to look beyond material objects. When we take the time to enjoy the people in our lives, we find true happiness. The memories that we make through sharing with others are priceless; we cannot put a value on them.

Create: The students will close their eyes and think about a favorite memory. What were they doing to make this memory so special, and who were they with? Let them describe that memory with all their senses. Maybe it was a party, a trip, a special visitor, or a vacation. The students will draw a picture showing this memory and write several sentences to explain the details of it.

There might be an opportunity to create a special moment in time with each other as a class. Once they have finished their drawing, move the class around to help create an ambiance that is comfortable and open. The goal is to encourage them to tell each other the stories of those cherished moments in their life, meanwhile creating a cherished moment in time right there in the classroom!

Reflect: As they share their memories, encourage students to ask each other questions about their special memory. Talk about whether each memory included material objects, experiences that they had, or both. We tend to remember and value experiences more than material objects. Encourage the students to reflect upon how they use their time. Could their time be better spent making everlasting memories by developing their relationships?

 Willpower

Students should walk away from this lesson inspired to put greater value on their time. They can use it to be with people they love and appreciate, to create wonderful experiences and memories, and to further their personal development and growth.

Lesson 28

Materials
My Best Me textbook, writing utensils, paper, markers, crayons, access to Internet

Resources
Student Worksheet: 4yu.info/?i=98428
Parent Summary: 4yu.info/?i=98478

Glossary
producer, consumer, economy, goods, service, taxes, utilized, demand, supply, service provider, bartering, exchange,

Motivation
There is a fine balance between the roles producers (supply) and consumers (demand) have in the economy. When we use services in our community or buy goods from a market or store, we are helping our economy grow. These interactions are valuable for students to understand.

Such growth can only happen, however, if there is cash flow in a nation. Many businesses provide a service for consumers, which generates an income. The money the provider receives in return is then used to buy their necessary goods or services. This is how a healthy economy works. In this lesson, students will discover their potential as a producer by finding opportunities to provide goods and services for others, such as walking a neighbor's dog, shoveling snow, or making and selling snacks or crafts. In exchange for their services, they may receive money or other goods or services. With the money they earn, they can buy items from the store, which turns them into a consumer, supporting a business.

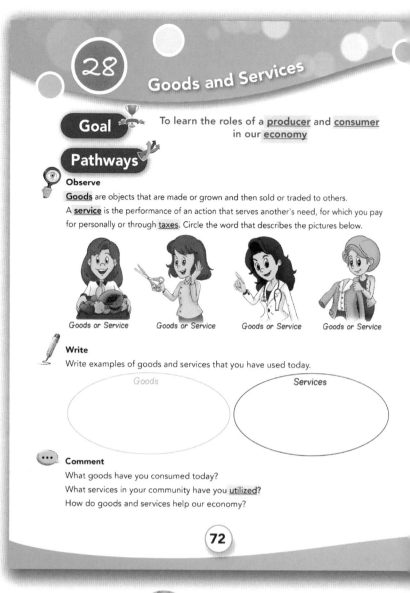

Goal

Students will learn the roles of producers and consumers in the economy, and how they will contribute to the economy

Pathways

Observe: Invite students to give examples of goods and services. You can make two lists on the board. Next, the students will look at the pictures provided and decide whether each picture is an example of goods or a service. Once done, discuss each picture with the whole class. #1 - Could be both. The food are goods, the person could be a server. #2 - A person cutting hair provides a service. #3 - A doctor provides a service to their patients. #4 - Clothes are goods that we buy.

Write: The students will write down some goods

Understand

Each one of us is a consumer; a person who purchases goods, uses services and supports the economy. Our everyday needs put a <u>demand</u> on others who can <u>supply</u> that need. This supply-and-demand interaction is what helps support the economy in our community. When we buy goods, we support the person or company that provides the product. When we go to a clinic, school, mechanic, or veterinarian, we pay for that service. The person who provides the goods is a producer. The person who provides a service is a <u>service provider</u>.

Goods and services generally are obtained in exchange for money. However, at times, goods and services are exchanged for other goods and services; this is called <u>bartering</u>. For example, if you grow apples on your farm you might give someone apples in <u>exchange</u> for a tune up for your car. In this situation, both people benefit and no money is exchanged.

Create

Think about the needs and desires in your community. Think about your skills and interests; how can they fit your community's demands? Do you have any goods or services that you could provide for others? Create a flyer to advertise your goods or services.

Dog Walking!

Reflect

How can you be a producer now?
Could you be a service provider? Please explain.
How do you benefit from providing your goods or services to others?
How do others benefit from your goods or services?
What is a need you see and think that people have that is not being provided?
What can you do to fulfill that need?

Willpower

I understand the role of consumers and producers in my community and their importance to the economy.

73

and services that they have consumed/used today, and draw lines coming off of the circle to make a "mind map." Some examples of goods they might have consumed are the foods they ate for breakfast, their lunch items, or the backpack they carry to school. Their parent or guardian may have even stopped for gas (a good) that morning. Services might have been provided by a bus driver, teacher, librarian, custodian, crossing guard, or even a cashier if they stopped at a store on the way to school.

Comment: Allow the students to share the list of goods they consumed, or services they received. It will surprise them how many services they receive during a day and how often goods and services go hand in hand. Discuss how these goods and services impact the local economy. Ask students how the money flows and tracks when they buy the food for their meals. Next, discuss how services help our economy. For example, a teacher is generally paid through the taxes we contribute to service us by teaching. The teacher now has money to buy goods and services from others in the community. This is how the economy works.

 Understand: Everyone is a consumer; a person who purchases goods or uses services. Although a consumer plays an important role in the economy, our goal in life should not be to only be a consumer. We should strive to be creative and find a way to provide for the needs and desires of others. Consumers as well as producers are needed for a healthy economy and society.

Sometimes people barter or exchange their goods and services for the goods and services they need. For example, if your family has a friend who paints houses, and your family fixes cars, you might do an exchange. Does anyone in your class have a parent who owns a business?

Create: Producers and providers focus on the needs and desires of the people around them, which stimulates them to make or offer things the community needs. Once they provide a needed service or desire of others, they will receive in exchange the things they need. Guide the students to think creatively about the needs and desires in their community. Then encourage them to consider how their skills and interests can produce and/or provide the goods and/or services others are looking for. The students will then create a poster advertising the service that they will provide. Make sure they add all the details about their service (i.e., clear description of service, cost, hours they can work, etc.)

Reflect: The students can share their goods and service ideas with each other. Discuss how providing the service will benefit others. Help them understand that even at a young age, they can play a role in their community's economy. Challenge your students to go out and produce goods or services.

Willpower

Students will understand their role in the economy. They will learn the influence and great value they can have as producers and providers in their local economy.

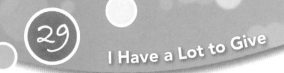

Lesson 29

Materials
My Best Me textbook, writing utensils, paper, markers, crayons

Resources
Student Worksheet: 4yu.info/?i=98429
Parent Summary: 4yu.info/?i=98479

Glossary
affection, encouraging words, fulfillment

Motivation
There are many ways that we are able to give gifts to others that do not involve money. Students should discover the great variety of priceless gifts that they have and can share with others (i.e., very valuable, but not expensive.) Another discovery is the sheer joy of giving, both for the individual receiving the gift and the one giving it.

Young children usually do not have money to spend on others, but they can give and serve others with who they are and what they can do. Children can give their time, attention, effort, services, love and affection to others. These gifts have the same impact as a wrapped present. This implies taking on responsibility; which, when broken down, contains two important words: RESPONSE and ABILITY. As students discover their abilities, they can learn to respond to what is going on around them: giving, sharing and serving others. In doing so, the students will experience joy, fulfillment, and satisfaction.

Life takes on a whole other dimension and meaning when we are focused on what we can do and give to others. New experiences, opportunities, connections, etc. find place when we are ready to give be it in season or out of season (when it suits us or when it does not suit us). Often others will need or ask for help from us at the most inconvenient moments. Students should learn to not draw back, but to manage everything in such a manner that giving to others will always be a priority. Giving should become a habit in their lives.

29 I Have a Lot to Give

 Goal To discover what I have to give, and learn to give what I have

Pathways

 Observe
There are many ways we can give to others. Look at the pictures below.

 Comment
What gift does each person give?
Does what they give cost them money?
Have you ever received anything that did not cost money? What was it?

Understand
We might tend to think that the best way to help others is to give money, objects or food. Although that can be helpful, not everyone has the ability to give in that manner. Fortunately, there are many other ways to give that can have the same or greater impact. We can give to others by donating our time, services, love, <u>affection</u>, <u>encouraging words</u> and acts of kindness.

The ways to give listed above cost no money for the giver, but they make a substantial impact on the receiver. When we learn how much we have to give, and start giving to those around us, we impact our community. Sharing our gifts of kindness with family, friends, and strangers also gives us joy and <u>fulfillment</u> in life.

74

 Goal

Students will discover how much they have to give, and learn to give what they have, particularly things that do not involve money, objects, or food

 **Pathways**

Observe: Discuss each of the pictures from the workbook in small groups or as a class. In these pictures, you see people giving their time, affection, effort, tokens or gifts, and their skills. What might students be able to give to the people around them as well as strangers, and how would they do so in a wise and safe manner?

Comment: Discuss with the students different ways of giving. In the images, we can see gifts such as management skills, relating and interacting with others, physical abilities like strength, effort, time, love, affection,

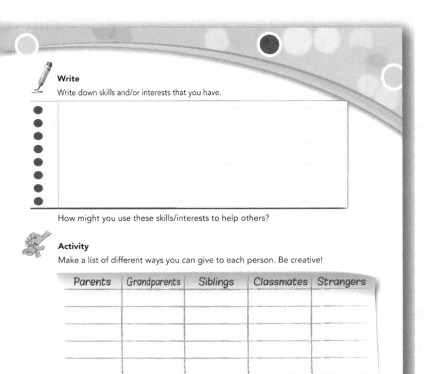

✏️ **Write**
Write down skills and/or interests that you have.

How might you use these skills/interests to help others?

✊ **Activity**
Make a list of different ways you can give to each person. Be creative!

Parents	Grandparents	Siblings	Classmates	Strangers

💭 **Reflect**
I know what I have to give. How am I going to give on a daily basis to help others?
Do I think it will be difficult at times to give to others? Why?
What personal valuable benefits will I receive from giving to others?

Willpower
I recognize the abundance I have to give and I am always ready to give it.

75

a smile, laughter, a story, handmade crafts and cards, etc.

Have students share the money-less gifts they receive; all the things their parents do for them, things they receive at school, etc. They might tend to think these gifts are a right, rather than a privilege. Have them think of a child who perhaps does not have parents, or children who do not have an opportunity to go to school. Be sure to tread thoughtfully regarding children who might be less privileged than your students. (Perhaps some students in your class live in such a situation.)

How does it feel when we are given something? Often, giving a gift is just as exciting as receiving one. It makes us feel wonderful in our hearts when we are able to give something meaningful to someone we love or care for. For instance, in the pictures, it did not cost anything to make another person feel appreciated and happy; it simply took thoughtfulness, effort and ability.

💡 **Understand:** At times, giving money or a present can be a meaningful way of giving, but it is not the only way that we can give. Fortunately, we can give to others by donating our time, services, love and affection, compliments or encouraging words, or even gifts from the heart. When we touch others with these "priceless" gifts, we make them feel appreciated. The benefit for the giver is satisfaction.

Giving might not always feel comfortable as it can interrupt what you want to do and when you want to do it. Giving implies making the other person more important than yourself (in a healthy way), and doing something when it best serves them and least serves you. Giving can imply some kind of sacrifice, but not in a negative way. It is the act of giving up something in order to give something to someone else.

✏️ **Write:** Students will think of ways that they are able to give to others. They can reflect on their skills and abilities and how they can use them to give something.

✊ **Activity:** The students will fill in the table with ways that they can give to the people mentioned. Have the students think about the person to whom they are giving. Of course, the subject on how to give to strangers is one that will need wisdom and caution. We want our students to be aware of their communities and the needs strangers have around them, responding in friendly and polite ways, yet in such a manner that they are safe and secure.

💭 **Reflect:** Let students share with each other ways that they are able to give. Invite the students to share how they feel, knowing that they have so much to give to others. Challenge them to put some of their ideas into action on a daily basis. By doing so, they help create a friendlier environment around them and their satisfaction in life increases.

Willpower

Students understand creative ways of how they can give to others daily of their time, talents, and treasure (financial or otherwise) and the great benefit they receive by doing so.

Lesson 30

Materials
My Best Me textbook, writing utensils, paper, markers, crayons, dictionary

Resources
Student Worksheet: 4yu.info/?i=98430
Parent Summary: 4yu.info/?i=98480

Glossary
qualities, leader, coach, aggressive, persistent, passionate, empathetic, disciplined, loyal, supportive, discerning, inspirational, integrity, determined, accountable

Motivation

A leader is a person who guides or organizes individuals or a group to accomplish a vision or set of objectives. Students will discover the qualities of an effective leader, so they can begin to take on and develop leadership roles. In order to be successful, students must learn to work cooperatively with others, follow instructions as well as give instructions. A great leader knows how to be a great follower, because they know what it takes in effort, time, and responsibility to be a leader. In order to work cooperatively, a person must know how to be a leader in a group, and allow others to operate in a leadership role as well.

A leader is focused on helping others become successful, no matter what. They support and lead others by their inspiring example. Students should learn how to lead without being bossy or aggressive. In order to get others to understand us, we must first earn their respect. This happens when their words line up with their actions.

The best leaders are those who do not have to give orders, but rather, inspire others to focus on the vision and/or objective. True leaders are able to develop a passion and internal motivation in those they lead to make the right choices and to do the things that advance the vision, even when it is uncomfortable and challenging. The sights of a leader should be on what lays ahead and not on who is following; yet, their primary interest should be the advancement and development of human capital.

---

30 I Am a Leader

Goal — To understand the qualities of an effective leader

Pathways

Observe

A leader is a person who guides and directs an individual or a group using organizational and other skills. In this image, we see a coach who is a leader of a soccer team. Write some words that you would use to describe a leader.

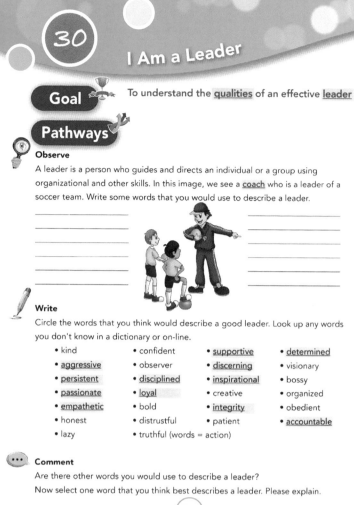

_____   _____
_____   _____
_____   _____
_____   _____

Write

Circle the words that you think would describe a good leader. Look up any words you don't know in a dictionary or on-line.

- kind
- aggressive
- persistent
- passionate
- empathetic
- honest
- lazy

- confident
- observer
- disciplined
- loyal
- bold
- distrustful
- truthful (words = action)

- supportive
- discerning
- inspirational
- creative
- integrity
- patient

- determined
- visionary
- bossy
- organized
- obedient
- accountable

 Comment

Are there other words you would use to describe a leader?
Now select one word that you think best describes a leader. Please explain.

76

Goal

Students will discover that they are able to lead and to do so effectively will require them to develop certain character traits

Pathways

Observe: Students will write words to describe a coach who has impact and influence. Most students will have experience working with a coach, tutor or trainer. The students can share their experiences, both positive and negative, about individuals who train them.

Write: Students will discover what describes a good leader. All of the words can be circled (except bossy, distrustful, aggressive and lazy). If a student has a different answer, encourage them to justify their answer and even add words that they think are missing. Invite

Understand

"A leader is a person who knows the way, goes the way, and shows the way." - John Maxwell

A leader is someone who is capable of guiding others to success and generally leads by example. A leader might be a parent at home, a boss at a job, the teacher in a classroom, a coach of a sports team, or a student on the playground. A leader is fully focused and dedicated to helping others achieve their goals. To be an effective leader, we must be able to get others to listen, understand, and follow our example without being bossy or aggressive. Both adults and children can be leaders. A child that organizes a soccer game at recess is leading classmates.

Activity - Share

What skills or talents do you have that you could use to lead others in developing themselves, such as dribbling a basketball or drawing a picture? Your task is to teach a skill to one or more of your peers. Remember to apply the qualities of an effective leader as you lead your group. I will lead one or more of my peers in: _____
_____ .

Reflect

What qualities of an effective leader did I discover in myself?
Is it difficult, challenging or even scary to lead classmates? Please explain.
How did I handle a situation that did not go according to my plan?
Are there any areas that I can improve to become a better leader?
Am I capable and humble to follow the leadership of another classmate? Why?

Willpower

I am a leader and will develop
the qualities of a successful leader.

77

---

organize the group and take action? When leading, it is important to be respectful and understanding of the other group members.

 Activity: Students will think of a skill they are confident in and would be able to teach to others. When we are confident, we are able to be better leaders. This might be a skill in a certain sport, such as dribbling a basketball or throwing a football, or a skill such as drawing or crafting. The goal of this activity is for the students to practice leading a group by teaching their particular skill. To do this, the leader must demonstrate leadership skills as described above, in order to successfully teach their group. It might be a good idea to review the attributes of a good leader.

Reflect: After each student has the opportunity to lead, talk about how the experience went for each group. Was the leader able to successfully teach their group a new skill? A part of being a good leader is the ability to adapt to the needs of your group. Did any of the leaders need to adjust their plan to meet the needs of the group? Were any of the groups unsuccessful? It is important to always look for successes, but also to reflect on things that might go better next time. Encourage your students to look for at least one area that they can improve upon. As teachers, we can relate to this on a daily basis. Many lessons do not go as planned, and we have to reevaluate our teaching and adjust our lessons to make them better. Sharing from your personal experience may encourage the students to explore and seek ways in which they can improve.

students to reflect on and share their experiences, both as being a leader and follower.

Comment: Divide the students into small groups and have them discuss why they thought each word did or did not describe a good leader. Then have each group decide together which is the most important quality for a leader to have. The team will need to agree on one word and be able to defend why they chose that word.

Understand: Read this section with your students and invite them to reflect on and share their experiences, both being a leader and following another's lead. In order for any leader to be successful, they need others to want to follow them and work positively and effectively with them leading. Ask students to think of activities when they have worked in a group in class, on the playground, or at home. Was there one person who took the lead? How did that go? How did the leader act? What did the leader do? What was the result?

Ask your students what happens if there is no leader. Can the group achieve success if no one takes the lead to

Willpower

The students will understand the qualities of effective leadership and use these skills to step up as a leader.

Glossary

Accomplished: a completed state (#40)

Accomplishments: special skill or ability acquired by practice (#15)

Accountable: taking responsibility (#76)

Acrostic: a word written vertically, each letter begins a word or sentence (#25)

Achieving: to accomplish a goal (#14)

Adopting: choose to be a provider of care for something or someone (#65)

Advantage: to benefit or gain (#19)

Affection: feeling of liking and caring for something or someone (#74)

Affects: produces a change in (#30)

Aggressive: having driving forceful energy (#76)

Alternative: a different choice (#20)

Analyze: to evaluate or examine (#23)

Anxious: uncomfortable or uncertain (#41)

Appreciate: to value highly, gratitude (#12)

Approach: to draw closer to (#31)

Assumption: something taken as being true or factual (#32)

Astute: to understand things clearly (#52)

Attentively: act of paying close attention (#61)

Attractive: appealing or welcoming (#29)

Bartering: exchanging goods and services without money (#73)

Betrayed: abandoned, mistreated or violated trust (#50)

Bifocal glasses: corrects near vision and corrects distant vision (#18)

Billion: a number equal to 1,000 million (#63)

Broader: extension from side to side (#65)

Brochures: a pamphlet or booklet (#49)

Burdens: duties or responsibilities (#54)

Caffeine: substance found in coffee and tea that makes a person feel more alert (#35)

Calories: energy-producing food aspect (#36)

Caution: care taken to avoid trouble or danger (#37)

Cement: something serving to unite firmly and permanently (#32)

Chain reaction: a series of events; each event causing the next one (#66)

Characteristic: a defining trait or quality (#45)

Chart: information given in a list or table (#22)

Chef: a skilled professional cook (#14)

Chemical: substance produced in the body that has a particular effect (#12)

Coach: one who helps another develop a skill (#76)

Collaboratively: working with others (#47)

Comfortable: physically at ease (#39)

Committed: make a promise to someone (#37)

Commitment: something pledged (#37)

Common: similar aspect found among many members (#44)

Communicate: to convey information (#20)

Compare: find similarity or differences (#41)

Comparing: examining for similarity or differences (#44)

Complex: hard to separate or solve (#32)

Complimenting: expressing respect, admiration and best wishes (#57)

Concentrate: to focus attention on (#47)

Confidence: the state of being certain (#29)

Confidentiality: being trustworthy with someone else's secrets (#11)

Conflict: an extended struggle or a clashing disagreement (#54)

Conscious: awake and able to understand what is happening around you (#23)

Consider: to think about carefully (#35)

Considerate: thoughtful of the rights and feelings of others (#56)

Considered: careful thought (#65)

Constructive: promoting improvement or development (#30)

Consume: to use up (#34)

Consumer: people who buy things (#72)

Contrasting: noticeable differences (#44)

Contributes: plays a significant part in a result (#47)

Convince: to argue as to make a person agree or believe (#29)

Cooperate: to act or work together to get something done (#23)

Cope: to deal with and try to find solutions for problems (#31)

Create: to produce something from nothing, to speak invisible things like thoughts, ideas and imaginations into existence. Words frame our reality. (#4)

Creatures: beings created either animate or inanimate (#64)

Credit: accounting an accomplished task to someone (#38)

Critical: likely or eager to find fault (#23)

Culture: set of shared attitudes, values and goals (#45)

Cyberworld: the computer world; Internet (#53)

Damage: to cause harm or loss to (#63)

Decisively: act of causing something to end in a certain way (#17)

Defeated: to lose (#17)

Deforestation: the action of cutting down trees and clearing the forest (#66)

Demand: requiring a product or service (#73)

Designing: thinking up and planning out in the mind (#47)

Destiny: a determined course of events (#14)

Determination: direction or tendency to a certain end (#17)

Determined: having made a firm decision and being resolved not to change it. (#74) (#76)

Diet: food and drink regularly provided or consumed (#35)

Diminish: to become gradually less or smaller (#63)

Discerning: knowing the difference between justice and injustice (#76)

Discharge: release (#36)

Disciplined: sticking to rules of behavior (#76)

Discussed: talked about (#54)

Dominant: controlling or being more powerful or important than all others (#23)

Domino effect: when one event causes other events to happen (#17)

Donating: giving to help people in need (#57)

Dynamic: an underlying cause of change or growth (#44)

Economy: the exchange of money in society (#72)

Effectively: being able to produce something that meets a goal (#20)

Efficient: bringing about a desired result with little waste (#47)

Efficiently: in a manner that brings about a desired result with little waste (#23)

Electronics: devices powered by electricity (#70)

Eliminate: to remove or take away someone or something (#29)

Eliminating: getting rid of (#29)

Embarrassed: feeling or showing self-conscious confusion and distress (#13)

Empathetic: knowing how others feel (#76)

Encouraging words: to build up in strength or desire (#74)

Endangered: close to becoming extinct (#66)

Engaged: promised to be married or busy with activity (#21)

Environment: the conditions by which one is surrounded (#60)

Envision: to imagine something(#60)

Excel: to be superior in some respect (#14)

Exchange: to put one thing in place of another (#73)

Excuse: to make apology for (#55)

Explore: to go into for purposes of discovery or adventure (#49)

Expressions: looks on someones face; also, meaningful words or sayings (#57)

Extent: the distance or range that is covered (#60)

Extinct: no longer existing (#66)

Family: a unit consisting of parents and children living together, there are different formations of family units, it should be a safe place. (#4)

Fertilize: to give plants extra nutrients to grow and develop (#34)

Fixed Mindset: a mental attitude not willing to change (#31)

Flavors: qualities of something that affects the taste (#14)

Focus: an adjustment that gives clear vision (#41)

Focused: clear concentrated perception (#21)

Food coloring: food die or pigment (#35)

Fortunately: working out in a good way (#67)

Foster: to protect and take care of (#36)

Fulfillment: feeling of satisfaction and rightness (#74)

Gear: to make ready for operation (#21)

Goods: something offered for sale (#72)

Gratefulness: act of feeling or showing thanks (#61)

Grit: firmness of mind or spirit (#17)

Growth Mindset: a belief in the ability to learn and develop skills (#19)

Gymnastics: physical exercises designed to develop strength and coordination (#32)

Habitat: the place where a plant or animal naturally lives and grows (#66)

Harmony: in accord or agreement (#44)

Harshly: acting severely or cruelly (#37)

Hormones: chemicals that tell cells and body parts to do certain things (#12)

Hydrated: supplied with ample fluid or moisture (#64)

Hygiene: practices (such as cleanliness) necessary for health (#28)

Identifying: finding out or discovering who or what something is (#14)

Impact: a strong effect (#60)

Impressive: having the power to draw attention, awe or admiration (#44)

Increases: makes greater (#57)

Inevitable: sure to happen (#31)

Initiative: getting something started (#17)

Insecure: not confident (#13)

Inspirational: to motivate (#76)

Integrity: keeping a code of values (#76)

Intelligence: the ability to learn (#32)

Interact: to talk or do things with others (#50)

Interaction: an occasion when two or more people or things communicate with or react to each other (#64)

Internet: a worldwide system of connected networks (#52)

Interview: a meeting where Information is obtained through questions (#21)

Intimidating: producing feelings of fear or insecurity (#31)

Intuitive: readily learned or understood (#23)

Invigorates: gives life or energy to (#36)

Irreplaceable: unable to be replaced (#24)

Item: An individual article or unit, one that is part of a list or set (#70)

Judge: to form an opinion after careful consideration (#37)

Jump-start: to impart fresh or renewed energy to; energize (#41)

Kindness: the quality of being gentle and considerate (#56)

Label: words used to describe or identify (#48)

Leader: a person who guides others (#76)

Leadership: to lead, to administrate, to manage, to go before, the action of leading a group of people, the ability to influence others through words and deeds. (#4)

Leaning: bending and resting on; depending (#18)

Limits: prescribed maximum or minimum amounts (#53)

Logging: making an official record of (#53)

Long-term: lasting for a long period of time (#15)

Love: a personal decision to give the best you have for the wellbeing of another, independent of merit and without expecting anything in return (#4)

Loyal: faithful and trustworthy (#76)

Manufactured: something made from raw materials by hand or by machinery (#35)

Masterpiece: something done or made with exceptional skill (#24)

Maturing: growing and developing (#13)

Measure: a certain amount (#70)

Measuring tape: a device marked with units of length used to size objects or spaces (#46)

Mechanics: the person who works on machines (#49)

Memories: thoughts of past experiences (#71)

Modest: small or lesser (#37)

Moist: slightly wet (#28)

Momentum: the force that something in motion has because of its weight (#17)

Monitor: to check for a special reason (#53)

Motivate: a reason for doing something (#40) (#41)

Nourish: to cause to grow in a healthy state providing enough nutrients (#15)

Nutrients: substances needed for healthy growth and development (#15)

Odors: scents or smells; usually bad (#28)

Offensive: causing displeasure or resentment (#29)

Optimistic: expecting great things (#30)

Origami: folding paper into 3-dimensional figures without using scissors or glue (#20)

Originate: to bring into being (#45)

Overcomer: someone who gains control of something with great effort (#19)

Passionate: caring deeply about (#76)

Passive: not taking an active part (#16)

Persevere: to carry on in spite of opposition or discouragement (#18)

Persistent: never quitting (#76)

Personality: the unique innate traits of a human being (#22)

Personality traits: a set of traits specific to an individual (#18)

Perspective: determining what is important and what is not (#31)

Persuasive: the ability to change how people think (#65)

Phrase: words that express a single idea (63)

Planet: a large heavenly body that orbits a star (#24)

Possessions: something owned (#70)

Postpone: to put off until a later time (#17)

Potential: a quality that something has that can be developed to make it better (#32)

Precious: high emotional attachments (#71)

Preservatives: substances added to food to keep it from spoiling (#35)

Preventative: avoid something (#64)

Priceless: unable to put a price on (#71)

Prioritize: to put in order of importance (#41)

Privacy: freedom from unauthorized intrusion (#52)

Proactive: acting in anticipation of future problems or changes (#16) (#41)

Processed: prepared according to a routine (#35)

Procrastination: to keep putting off something that should be done (#16)

Produce: to generate, to make, to yield or give results, small things can produce great results, for example a seed is the image of a plant, but not just one plant, acres of plants or trees. (#4)

Producer: company or person who makes items for sale (#72)

Productively: successful results (#49)

Programmed: a set of instructions that can't be changed (#32)

Prohibit: to forbid by authority (#67)

Promotes: helps to succeed (#36)

Promptly: without delay, quickly, immediately (#16)

Properly: aligning to social or moral rules; correct action (#65)

Proportions: parts of the whole (#35)

Proteins: a muscle building nutrient found in food (meat, nuts, beans, milk, eggs) (#35)

Public server: computer company that provides access to the Internet (#52)

Purchase: to obtain by paying money (#65)

Purpose: the reason for which something is done, created or exists, it gives direction and meaning. Purpose is why we have destiny. Purpose gives intention and avoids abuse and misuse. (#4)

Putty: dough-like material (#33)

Qualities: good characteristics or traits (#76)

Reasonings: the ability of the mind to think and understand in a logical way (#41)

Recipes: instructions for making something by combining ingredients (#14)

Recognize: to know an remember upon seeing (#34)

Recommended: introduced or mentioned as being fit or worthy (#37)

Recycling: adapting to a new use (#62)

Reducing: making smaller or less (#62)

Refined: purified, precise; exact (#35)

Relaying: passing along by stages (#20)

Release: to set free or let go of (#54)

Religion: the belief in and worship of God or gods (#45)

Research: to search or investigate thoroughly (#52)

Resolve: to find an answer to; solve (#54)

Resource: a source of supply or support (#52)

Respectfully: act of having high or special regard for someone (#56)

Responsibilities: duties or tasks that you are required or expected to do (#13)

Reusing: using again (#62)

Reward: pleasant gift given for a service or accomplishment (41)

Roles: parts played by actors (#48)

Safekeeping: protect from danger, loss (#15)

Saturated fat: grease that is solid at room temperature (#35)

Scenario: a sequence of events especially when imagined (#39)

Sequence: a group of things that come one after another (#12)

Series: a number of things arranged in order (#15)

Service: something done for money (#72)

Service provider: someone that fulfills needs in exchange for money (#73)

Shelter: a place that covers or protects (#64)

Short-term: occurring over a relatively short period of time (#15)

Significant: a special or hidden meaning (#61)

Similarities: aspects that are alike (#44)

Skill: a developed or acquired ability (#38)

Sociable: liking to be around other people; friendly (#23)

Stress-free: free from physical or emotional tension (#41)

Stressful: feeling physical or emotional tension (#38)

Stretch: extend or make long (33)

Stunning: unusually lovely or attractive; striking (#45)

Supply: meeting a need (#73)

Supportive: giving help or aid (#76)

Surroundings: the conditions or things in the area around an individual; environment (#60)

Survey: to gather information from; to poll (#22)

Survive: to remain alive; to continue to exist (#64)

Sustainable: able to last or continue for a long time (#63)

Symbol: a sign or something that stands for or suggests something else (#15)

Talents: special creative qualities and abilities (#14)

Tasks: pieces of work that have been assigned (#40)

Taxes: money collected by law by the government (#72)

Tendency: a natural or prevailing disposition toward something (#14)

Token: an outer sign; also, a symbolic action (#51)

Toxins: poisonous substance that is very unstable in human tissues (#28)

Traditions: beliefs or customs handed down from one generation to another (#45)

Transferring: causing to pass from one to another (#20)

Trust: having confidence in or relying on (#50)

Trustworthy: worthy of confidence (#51)

Uncomfortable: feeling discomfort or uneasiness (#39)

Undesirable: having qualities that are unpleasing or unwanted (#30)

Unique: being the only one of its kind (#23)

Unite: to come together, form a unit (#44)

Utilized: to make use of (#72)

Variations: amounts of changes and differences (#44)

Venn diagram: a visual tool that shows the relationship of groups by overlapping circles (#44)

Vision: the act or power of imagination (#41)

Vulnerable: open to attack or damage (#50)

Waste management: rubbish removal; the department of a city responsible for trash pick-up (#49)

Whiny: given to complaining; high pitched (#31)

Wisely: with wisdom; knowledge gained over time(#63)

Work: is activity involving mental or physical effort done in order to achieve a purpose, it is to serve. It is a way to share your unique strengths, abilities, knowledge and ideas with those around you, generally creating satisfaction within you. (#4)

GENERATION
WHY

INSPIRE. REVEAL. PURSUE.

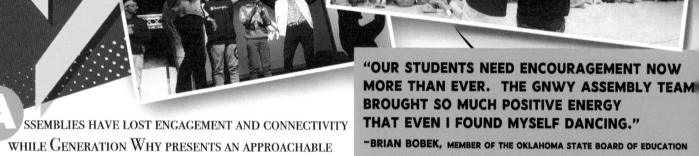

ASSEMBLIES HAVE LOST ENGAGEMENT AND CONNECTIVITY WHILE GENERATION WHY PRESENTS AN APPROACHABLE WAY TO DISCUSS SOME OF THE MOST DIFFICULT TOPICS STUDENTS ARE FACING IN THE REALM OF TRAUMA.

GENERATION WHY'S BLEND OF HIGH ENERGY, INSPIRING SPEAKING AND RELATABLE CREATIVE ARTS HAVE STUDENTS AND TEACHERS ON THE EDGE OF THEIR SEATS READY TO RECEIVE CHANGE AND HOPE.

HOPE EVOKES CHANGE AND CHANGE CAN BE THE TURNING POINT THAT MOVES A HEART IN A POSITIVE DIRECTION. GNWY USES RAPPERS, DANCERS, SPOKEN WORD ARTISTS AND MOTIVATIONAL SPEAKERS, THAT ENCOURAGE DIVERSITY, CULTURAL RELEVANCE, UNITY, AND SCHOOL BODY, STUDENT WIDE EMPOWERMENT.

THROUGH AN ASSEMBLY / PERFORMANCE / PRESENTATION, YOU ARE MOVED NOT ONLY PHYSICALLY, BUT EMOTIONALLY TOWARD A HEALTHIER YOU THROUGH CONVERSATIONS, RELATIONSHIPS AND ULTIMATELY, A HEALTHIER SCHOOL COMMUNITY.

"OUR STUDENTS NEED ENCOURAGEMENT NOW MORE THAN EVER. THE GNWY ASSEMBLY TEAM BROUGHT SO MUCH POSITIVE ENERGY THAT EVEN I FOUND MYSELF DANCING."
-BRIAN BOBEK, MEMBER OF THE OKLAHOMA STATE BOARD OF EDUCATION

"GENERATION WHY IS A BURST OF ENERGY AND ENCOURAGEMENT. THEY ARE CREATIVE STORYTELLERS AND ARTISTS THAT HAVE TURNED THEIR TRAUMAS INTO TRIUMPHS AND NOW USE THEIR GIFTS AND TALENTS TO INSPIRE TODAY'S YOUTH! I AM SO GRATEFUL FOR THEIR LEADERSHIP IN OUR COMMUNITY."
-ASHLEY HOGGATT, PRINCIPAL, DD KIRKLAND ELEMENTARY; BOARD MEMBER, OKLAHOMA ADMINISTRATOR FOR ELEMENTARY PRINCIPALS

WWW.PURSUEYOURWHY.ORG

CONTACT: GNWY@FIGHTFORTHEFORGOTTEN.ORG

EMPOWERED BY: